Mixer Cook Book

Dear Readers,

To become the proud owner of a mixer is a great day in the life of any cook. To own a liquidiser, as well, is a luxury indeed.

This book has been devised to help you use your mixer and/or liquidiser to the best possible advantage. It speeds up your cooking, can make delicious treats like home-made mayonnaise and light-as-a-feather sponge cakes an everyday affair and can give you the equivalent of another pair of hands in the kitchen.

Once you have come to terms with your mixer, you will be able to shortcut your cooking with ease, even when using conventional cookery recipes.

Yours sincerely,

The Editor

CONTENTS

Uses of Mixers and Liquidisers

Mixers and liquidisers have been available for several years, but, until recently, they were expensive. Now, many more makes are on the market, and an efficient machine can be bought at a reasonable price. This book has been written to show you how to get the best use from the machine of your choice.

Naturally, the larger the machine the more uses it will have. However, correctly used, it is amazing the help that even a quite small and inexpensive machine can give in the kitchen. In this book, you will find a few recipes that are impracticable without the aid of a liquidiser or mixer. Most of the recipes, however, are everyday favourites, which, with the use of one of these modern 'kitchen aids', are made more quickly than when using the conventional wooden spoon or sieve!

You don't need special recipes to use your mixer or liquidiser: it's only the method of preparation that sometimes differs. Check our Basic Recipe chapter and adapt the preparation of your own favourite family recipes. After preparing most of the other recipes in the book, you will see ways of adapting many of the recipes we publish each month in FAMILY CIRCLE.

Remember, your mixer or liquidiser is an electrical appliance: take care not to get the motor wet, or stand the machine on a wet surface. Do not overwork the appliance; follow the times the manufacturer recommends for its continuous working. Usually, mixers should not be run for more than 5 minutes without a break, and liquidisers for not more than 45 to 60 seconds; this should be quite long enough to complete mixing or blending. For convenience, keep your appliance on the kitchen worktop.

It is important, before using your mixer or liquidiser, to read the manufacturer's instructions very carefully, as different makes vary in design.

Mixers
Use your mixer for rubbing-in mixtures, creaming, whisking and kneading, as for bread. Many makes have different beater attachments designed for different mixtures. When following the recipes in this book, always use the attachment recommended by the manufacturer for the type of mixture.

When creaming butter and sugar together, it is advisable to fill mixer bowl with hot water, place beaters inside bowl and leave for a few minutes to warm them. Drain and dry bowl and beaters thoroughly; this will prevent creamed mixture sticking to beaters and sides of bowl. If your mixer has a choice of bowl size, or if it is a hand-held machine, choose the bowl size most suitable for amount of mixture.

In some cases, stand mixers need to be watched, or the mixture will not be properly mixed or creamed. Stop the machine, use a spatula or wooden spoon to scrape the mixture down from sides of bowl, then restart motor.

Generally, the lighter the mixture, the higher the speed required to do the job properly, and the smaller the quantity, the lower the speed required. But, be careful, you can overbeat mixtures. Cream will turn to butter, if you don't watch it carefully, and pastry will be difficult to handle, if over rubbed in. If your mixer has a choice of speeds, use the low speed for rubbed-in mixtures, like making pastry; medium speed for creamed mixtures, such as butter and sugar for cakes; and high speed for whisking egg white for meringue, for instance.

Liquidisers and Blenders
Use the liquidiser (or blender) for making smooth soups, drinks, purées for baby foods or special diets, batters. Use it for breadcrumbs, chopping vegetables and parsley, and grinding nuts, but check the

manufacturer's instructions, because, with some machines, you must use the grinder section for dry foods.

The liquidiser is so designed that the mixture in the goblet follows a pattern when the motor is running, the mixture being pushed up sides of goblet, then falling down the centre on to the blades. Don't let the liquidiser labour; if it appears to be making heavy weather of the mixture, or you can see that only the bottom half is being blended, add a little more liquid. Alternatively, stop the machine, scrape mixture down from sides of goblet on to blades, then restart the machine. NEVER put your hand or any type of tool into the liquidiser goblet while the motor is switched on.

Some liquidisers have a grinder attachment; this should be used in place of the liquidiser goblet for grinding nuts, chocolate and biscuits. Some manufacturers recommend that it be used for making breadcrumbs, as well.

Never overfill the liquidiser goblet; generally, it should be only half filled; soups and drinks should be divided into several batches, depending on size of goblet. When making thick pastes or pâtés, smaller batches should be placed in the goblet than when blending drinks: the heavier the mixture, the harder the motor has to work. Always cut the harder foods, like cheese, into $\frac{3}{4}$in dice before placing in liquidiser goblet. Larger pieces may get caught under blades and jam machine.

Always place lid on liquidiser before starting the motor. Some makes of liquidiser have a small cap in the lid, which may be removed while the motor is running for adding ingredients: more oil when making mayonnaise, for instance, or for dropping ingredients directly on to blades, as when making breadcrumbs. When you first switch on the machine, it is advisable to place a hand on the cover to avoid the possibility of the lid coming off under the first impact, and also to steady the machine.

Once again, it is essential to follow the manufacturer's instructions for the care of your make of liquidiser or mixer. Some need a little oil, from time to time, others will not need oiling. Keep all machines clean and avoid excessive heat.

Wipe the plastic parts of machine with a cloth that has been wrung out in hot, soapy water, and wipe dry with a tea towel. NEVER use harsh abrasives, strong detergents or washing soda. Wash mixer beaters and bowl in hot, soapy water, then rinse and dry thoroughly.

The liquidiser may be cleaned by placing a little hot water and liquid detergent in the goblet and running machine with lid on goblet for a few seconds, or by washing goblet in hot, soapy water; rinse and dry thoroughly. Do not place goblet in a dish-washing machine, as this may damage the seal, where the blades fit into the goblet.

The liquidiser goblet should not be exposed to sudden changes of temperature. Let boiling liquids cool slightly before placing in goblet, or add them to cold liquids.

Coding of Mixers and Liquidisers

When testing the recipes in this book, we used a wide variety of mixers and liquidisers. For our purpose, we divided them into six groups. Above each recipe, you will find numbers corresponding to the numbered symbol pictured; this will tell you if you can make the dish with your particular machine. In some recipes, both a liquidiser and mixer are used. However, you can still make the recipe if you own one of the required appliances and don't mind preparing the other part of the recipe by hand: for example, whisking egg whites or rubbing fat into flour.

1 Large mixers with stand and bowl: In this group are all the powerful mixers, often with many attachments. These mixers should be kept in a convenient place in the kitchen, as they are heavy to move about. They have their own bowl, or bowls that fit on to a rotating stand.

2 Liquidisers with a working capacity of $1\frac{1}{2}$ pints or over: These may be either an attachment to a mixer in Group 1 or a separate liquidiser with a motor of its own. They will quickly reduce many foods to a purée and will chop and grind a great variety of foods.

3 Small mixers with stand and bowl: These are the less powerful mixers. They are capable of doing almost as much as the larger mixers, but care should be taken that the motor is not overstressed. They are not strong enough to take heavy mixtures, nor can they cope with large quantities. Most of these machines may be detached from their stands and held by hand; this is particularly useful when it is necessary to beat a mixture in a pan or over hot water at the cooker.

4 Hand-held mixers: These mixers are very useful kitchen aids, their primary use being whisking, though they can be used for creaming and rubbing in. Because they need to be held all the time they are working, they have to be switched off before adding ingredients. Care must be taken not to overstrain the motor. Some mixers of this type only have one speed.

5 These small liquidisers are not as powerful as the larger ones and must only be switched on for a few seconds at a time, to avoid overheating the motor. If the machine has a grinder attachment, use this for chopping or grinding all dry ingredients. The liquidiser will not take stiff mixtures and may need more liquid added than with more powerful models. If you want to liquidise large quantities of food, divide it up and do a little at a time. It may be necessary to let the machine cool down between each session.

6 Wide-based liquidisers: These are of the more powerful type, but, because of their design, are not suitable for small quantities. They are ideal for drinks and soups. These large liquidisers may be used also for jobs not usually done in liquidisers: for example, rubbing fat into flour for pastry and cakes.

Basic Recipes

In this chapter, you will find all the usual basic recipes for pastry, cakes, icings, scones and sauces, but, for use with your mixer or liquidiser, the recipe methods differ from the conventional ways of mixing. Vary the flavours as you please, to make your own favourite recipes.

1 3 4   SHORTCRUST PASTRY

4oz plain flour
$\frac{1}{4}$ level teaspoon salt
1oz margarine
1oz lard or cooking fat
Cold water to mix

1 Place flour and salt in mixer bowl. Add fats, cut into pieces. Switch on mixer at low speed and run machine until mixture resembles fine breadcrumbs.
2 Add water (about 1 teaspoon for every 1oz flour) and mix with a fork; press together to form a firm dough. Roll out on a floured board; use as desired.
NOTE: It is not advisable to use mixer when adding water, or the dough will be very short and unmanageable.

1 3 4   PLAIN SCONES
(pictured on page 10)

Makes 8:
8oz plain flour
1 level teaspoon salt
1 level teaspoon bicarbonate of soda
2 level teaspoons cream of tartar
2 level teaspoons castor sugar
2oz margarine
Scant $\frac{1}{4}$ pint milk

1 Prepare a hot oven (450 deg F, Gas Mark 8). Grease a baking sheet.
2 Sift flour, salt, bicarbonate of soda, cream of tartar and sugar into mixer bowl. Add margarine, cut into pieces. Run machine at low speed until mixture resembles fine breadcrumbs.
3 Quickly stir in milk with a fork, to form a soft dough. If dough is dry, add a little extra milk. Turn out on to a floured board and knead lightly.
4 Roll out to a round, 1in thick; mark into 8 or cut in rounds. Place on baking sheet, brush with milk and bake, just above centre of oven, until risen and golden brown, 12 to 15 minutes.
NOTE: Scones may be made with 8oz self-raising flour; in this case, omit bicarbonate of soda and cream of tartar.

2 5 6   FRESH BREADCRUMBS

1 Remove crusts and break bread into pieces.
2 Place a little at a time in liquidiser goblet and run machine until bread is crumbed. (If liquidiser has a small cap in lid, machine may be switched on and bread dropped through lid directly on to blades.)
NOTE: Some manufacturers of liquidisers recommend that the grinder attachment be used for breadcrumbs.

1 3 4   DROP SCONES
(pictured on page 10)

Makes 12:
5oz plain flour
1 level teaspoon cream of tartar
$\frac{1}{2}$ level teaspoon bicarbonate of soda
1oz semolina
2oz castor sugar
1 standard egg
2 tablespoons cooking oil
4 tablespoons milk

1 Place all ingredients in the mixer bowl.
2 Run machine until mixture is smooth.
3 Heat and grease a griddle, solid electric hot-plate or thick frying pan, until moderately hot. (A spot of water should just sizzle when dropped on griddle.)
4 Drop tablespoonsful of the mixture on griddle, allowing room for scones to spread slightly. Cook until bubbles have risen to surface and burst. Turn over, press down on to hot griddle and cook until golden brown. When cooked, place in a folded napkin to keep moist. Serve with butter or whipped cream and jam.

1 3 4 6   ROCK BUNS

Makes 12:
1 standard egg
8oz self-raising flour (or 8oz plain flour and
   1 rounded teaspoon baking powder)
$\frac{1}{2}$ level teaspoon salt
4oz margarine
3oz castor sugar
2oz currants
Milk

1 Prepare a hot oven (450 deg F, Gas Mark 8). Grease a baking sheet. Beat egg. Place flour, baking powder (if used) and salt into mixer bowl. Add margarine, cut into small pieces.
2 Run machine at low speed until mixture resembles fine breadcrumbs. Stir in sugar and currants; add egg and mix to a stiff paste with a fork, adding a little milk, if necessary.
3 Using 2 forks, place mixture in rough heaps on baking sheet and cook for 10 to 15 minutes until firm and light brown. Remove from baking sheet and leave to cool on a wire rack.

1 3 4   SPONGE CAKE

2 standard eggs
2oz castor sugar
2oz plain flour
½ level teaspoon baking powder

1 Prepare a moderate oven (350 deg F, Gas Mark 4).
Brush 2 (7in) sandwich tins with oil or melted fat and line
each with a circle of greaseproof paper, then grease paper.
2 Place eggs and sugar together in a bowl and whisk at
high speed over a saucepan of hot water on the table until
mixture leaves a trail when mixer is switched off and lifted.
Remove bowl from pan and continue whisking until cool.
(If using a mixer with a stand and bowl, fill bowl with very
hot water, leave for a few minutes, then pour out water and
thoroughly dry bowl. Add eggs and sugar to bowl and
whisk at high speed until mixture is thick and cool.)
3 Sift flour and baking powder together, then carefully fold
into egg mixture with a metal spoon.
4 Pour into prepared tins and bake in centre of oven for 20
to 25 minutes. Test by pressing with the fingers. If cooked,
cakes should spring back, have stopped bubbling and have
begun to shrink from sides of tins.
5 Turn out, remove paper and leave to cool on a wire rack.
Sandwich cakes together with jam or jam and cream; dredge
with castor sugar.

---

1 3 4   MERINGUES

Makes 12 meringue shells:
2 egg whites
4oz castor sugar

1 Heat oven to lowest setting and place a shelf in coolest
position. Line a baking sheet with greaseproof paper and
brush lightly with cooking oil. Alternatively, use silicone-
treated paper, in which case oil is not necessary.
2 Place egg whites in mixer bowl, which should be clean
and grease free.
3 Whisk at highest speed until stiff, but not dry.
4 Whisk in half the sugar, then fold in remainder, cutting
through mixture with a metal spoon until all sugar has been
incorporated.
5 Fill a tablespoon with meringue and smooth it into a
mound from each side with a knife. Hold side of spoon on
baking sheet and carefully scoop meringue off with another
tablespoon. Repeat procedure to make 12 shells. Place in
oven and leave oven door slightly ajar.
6 Dry out for 3 to 5 hours. Meringues should easily lift off
paper. Leave to cool. Store in an air-tight tin until needed,
then fill with whipped cream and place in paper cake cases.

---

2 5 6   BASIC WHITE SAUCE

½ pint milk
1oz plain flour
Salt and pepper
1oz butter or margarine

1 Place milk and flour in liquidiser goblet; add seasonings.
Run machine until well blended.
2 Melt butter or margarine in a small saucepan. Add
contents of liquidiser goblet and stir over a moderate heat
until sauce comes to the boil. Simmer, stirring, for 2
minutes.

---

2 5 6   CRUMB CRUST

2oz butter
6oz digestive biscuits
2oz demerara sugar

1 Melt butter in a small saucepan. Place biscuits, a few at a
time, in grinder or liquidiser goblet and run machine until
biscuits are reduced to fine crumbs.
2 Place in a bowl and add demerara sugar and butter. Mix
well.
3 Press mixture into bottom and sides of a 7in pie plate.
Leave in a cool place to harden.

---

1 2 3 4 5 6

PANCAKE AND YORKSHIRE PUDDING BATTER

½ pint milk
1 standard egg
4oz plain flour
¼ level teaspoon salt

1 Place all ingredients in liquidiser goblet and run machine
until well mixed.
2 Cook as pancakes (see Seafood Pancakes, page 17)
or as a Yorkshire pudding.
NOTE: This batter may also be made with a mixer. Place half
the milk, egg, flour and salt in mixer bowl and mix at
medium speed until batter is smooth; mix in remaining milk
at low speed.

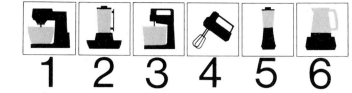

1 3 4   BUTTER ICING

2oz butter, softened
6oz icing sugar
1½ to 2 tablespoons top of the milk or liquid
   flavouring (coffee, orange juice, etc)

1 Place butter and icing sugar in mixer bowl.
2 Run machine at low speed, gradually beating in
flavouring. Use to fill or ice a cake.

---

1 3 4   GLACE ICING

4oz icing sugar
1 to 2 tablespoons water or flavouring

1 Place icing sugar in mixer bowl.
2 Run machine at low speed, gradually beating in liquid.
Spread on cake and leave to set.

---

1 3 4   ROYAL ICING

For sufficient icing to ice top and sides of a 7in round or a
6in square cake, with two coats of icing:
About 1¼lb icing sugar
3 egg whites
1 teaspoon clear honey or glycerine

1 Sieve icing sugar.
2 Put egg whites in a clean and grease-free mixer bowl.
Add sufficient icing sugar to mix to a consistency similar to
thick cream.
3 Beat for 5 to 7 minutes, until icing is stiff and stands up
in stiff points when beaters are stopped and lifted.
4 Beat in honey (or glycerine). Cover bowl with a damp
cloth and leave for 1 hour. Stir icing with a wooden spoon
to break down any bubbles. Adjust consistency with egg
white or lemon juice, for coating, if necessary.
For piping, add extra icing sugar.

---

1   AMERICAN FROSTING

2½ fluid oz water
8oz granulated sugar
1 egg white

1 Place water in a thick saucepan with granulated sugar
and heat slowly until dissolved. Boil until syrup forms a soft

ball when dropped in a saucer of cold water, or syrup
registers 240 deg F on a sugar thermometer.
2 Meanwhile, place egg white in a clean, grease-free mixer
bowl and whisk at top speed until stiff and dry. Pour on the
sugar syrup slowly, and continue whisking until mixture
stiffens and will form soft peaks.
3 Place cake on a plate; quickly spread frosting over and
make peaks with a round-bladed knife. Leave to set.

---

4   JIFFY AMERICAN FROSTING

6oz castor sugar
1 egg white
2 tablespoons hot water
Pinch of cream of tartar

1 Place all ingredients in a basin and place over a saucepan
of hot water. Whisk at high speed for about 5 minutes, until
mixture thickly coats back of spoon.
2 Pour over cake and leave to set.

---

2 6   BAKED EGG CUSTARD

For 4 portions:
3 large or 4 standard eggs
¾ pint milk
1oz castor sugar
½ teaspoon vanilla essence
A little grated nutmeg

1 Prepare a very cool oven (275 deg F, Gas Mark 1). Half
fill a roasting tin with warm water.
2 Place all ingredients, except nutmeg, in liquidiser goblet
and run machine until well mixed. Strain into a 1¼-pint
soufflé dish or pie dish. Sprinkle with grated nutmeg.
3 Place dish in tin containing water, and bake in centre of
oven for 1¼ hours or until set and lightly brown on top.
Remove dish from roasting tin and leave until custard is quite
cold (this takes about 3 hours). Loosen edge by pulling
towards centre gently with the fingers, and turn out on to a
serving plate.
Variations on Baked Custards
Caramel-flavoured Custard: Place 2oz granulated sugar and
2 tablespoons water in a small, thick saucepan and heat
slowly until sugar has dissolved; boil steadily, without
stirring, until sugar turns a deep golden brown. Add
unsweetened milk, a little at a time, and stir until caramel
dissolves. Add to eggs in liquidiser and run machine until
well blended. Strain into dish.
Coffee custard: Flavour milk with 2 rounded teaspoons of
instant coffee powder.

Pictured here are several old favourites which are quicker and easier to make, using a mixer or liquidiser. They are: Pinwheel Biscuits, biscuit shapes, sandwiched biscuits, Plain Scones, Iced Biscuits, Victoria Sandwich Cake, Lemon Meringue Pie, Drop Scones, Chocolate Swiss Roll and Plain Scone round

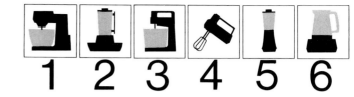

1 3 4   VICTORIA SANDWICH CAKE
(pictured left)
4oz butter or margarine
4oz castor sugar
2 standard eggs
4oz self-raising flour (or 4oz plain flour and 1 level teaspoon baking powder)
Jam
Icing or castor sugar

1 Prepare a moderate oven (375 deg F, Gas Mark 5). Brush 2 (7in) sandwich tins with oil or melted fat; line each with a circle of greaseproof paper and grease paper.
2 Fill mixer bowl with hot water and place beaters in bowl; leave for 2 minutes, empty bowl, then dry bowl and beaters. Place butter, cut in pieces, and sugar in mixer bowl and cream until mixture is light and fluffy. Add eggs, one at a time, beating well after each addition. Fold in flour and baking powder, if used, with a metal spoon.
3 Spread mixture evenly in tins and smooth with a spoon. Bake in centre of oven for 20 to 25 minutes.
4 Test by pressing with fingers. If cooked, cakes should spring back, have stopped bubbling and have begun to shrink from sides of tin. Turn out, remove paper and leave to cool on wire rack.
5 When cold, sandwich cakes together with jam and dredge top with icing or castor sugar.

---

1 3 4   SWISS ROLL
(pictured left)
2 standard eggs
2oz castor sugar
2oz plain flour
½ level teaspoon baking powder
2 tablespoons jam

1 Prepare a moderately hot oven (400 deg F, Gas Mark 6). Draw around base of an 11in by 7in Swiss-roll tin on greaseproof paper. Cut paper ½in out from line; crease paper on line. Grease tin and press paper down into tin, then grease paper.
2 Place eggs and sugar together in a bowl and whisk at high speed over a saucepan of hot water on the table until mixture leaves a trail when mixer is switched off and lifted. Remove bowl from pan and continue whisking until cool. (If using a mixer with a stand and bowl, fill bowl with very hot water, leave for a few minutes, then pour out water and thoroughly dry bowl. Add eggs and sugar to bowl and whisk at high speed until mixture is thick and cool.)
3 Sift flour and baking powder together, then carefully fold into egg mixture with a metal spoon.
4 Pour into prepared tin and shake tin gently to level

mixture. Bake in centre of oven for 8 to 10 minutes. Test by pressing with the fingers. If cooked, sponge should spring back, have stopped bubbling and have begun to shrink from sides of tin. While cake is baking, heat jam in a small saucepan and cut a piece of greaseproof paper about 1in bigger all round than tin; sprinkle thickly with sugar.
5 Invert cake on to sugared paper. Quickly loosen sides of paper on bottom of cake and carefully peel off.
6 Trim edges of cake with a sharp knife. Make a cut halfway through cake 1in from, and parallel with, the end from which cake will be rolled. Quickly spread cake with warmed jam, taking jam almost to cut edges.
7 To make a firm start to the roll, press half-cut edge down and hold with one hand; using the paper, roll cake firmly. Hold cake for a moment, with greaseproof paper around, to set cake. Remove paper and leave Swiss roll to cool on a wire rack.
NOTE: For Chocolate or Coffee Swiss Roll, replace ½oz flour with ½oz cocoa or add a level teaspoon of instant coffee powder to the egg and sugar mixture. Roll up without jam, but roll in the greaseproof paper. When cool, remove paper, unroll, and fill with vanilla, chocolate or coffee butter icing. (See recipe on page 9.)

---

1 3 4   BASIC BISCUIT MIXTURE

3oz margarine
3oz castor sugar
1 tablespoon milk
½ teaspoon vanilla essence
5oz plain flour
1oz cornflour
½ level teaspoon baking powder

DECORATION
Glacé Icing and Butter Icing (see recipes on page 9)
Silver balls; sugar strands; small jelly sweets

1 Prepare a moderately hot oven (400 deg F, Gas Mark 6). Grease 2 baking sheets.
2 Place margarine, cut in pieces, and sugar in mixer bowl. Run machine at low speed until mixture is light and fluffy. Mix in milk, vanilla essence, flour, cornflour and baking powder. Turn on to a floured board and knead until smooth.
3 Roll out on floured board to ⅛in thickness; cut into fancy shapes. Lift gently on to baking sheets.
4 Bake in centre of oven for about 8 minutes, or until biscuits are light golden at edges. Cool on a wire rack.
5 To decorate: Ice with Glacé Icing, then, while icing is still wet, decorate with silver balls, sugar strands or jelly sweets. Alternatively, when icing has set, pipe on Butter Icing, or sandwich 2 biscuits together with Butter Icing.

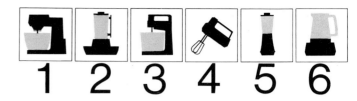

1 2 3 4 5 6

2 5 6   VEGETABLE SOUP

For 4 to 5 portions:
1 onion
1lb vegetables (carrots, leeks, sticks or leaves of
    celery, tomatoes)
1 large potato
1oz butter
1½ pints stock or 2 stock cubes and water
Milk (optional)
Salt and pepper

1 Prepare vegetables, according to kind, and slice. Place in
a large saucepan with butter and fry, stirring occasionally,
for about 10 minutes.
2 Add stock, bring to boil, cover and simmer until vegetables
are cooked.
3 Place in liquidiser goblet and run machine until smooth.
(Do not overfill liquidiser; divide soup into 2 or more
batches.) Rinse saucepan.
4 Pour soup into saucepan (strain if mixture is fibrous).
Adjust consistency with milk, if necessary. Bring to boil and
season to taste.
NOTE: A 'one variety' soup can be made from this recipe,
but add some celery or celery salt for additional flavour.

1 3 4   VANILLA ICE CREAM

For 6 portions:
1 level tablespoon custard powder
2 level tablespoons castor sugar
½ pint milk
1 teaspoon vanilla essence
1 (5 fluid oz) carton double cream

1 Turn refrigerator to coldest setting.
2 Place custard powder and sugar in a basin. Mix together
with a little cold milk.
3 Put remaining milk on to heat. Pour hot milk on to
blended custard powder. Return to pan and bring to boil,
stirring. Cook for 2 minutes.
4 Remove from heat and add vanilla essence. Cover with a
piece of dampened greaseproof paper and leave in a bowl of
cold water to cool.
5 Whisk cream lightly and fold into the cooled custard. Pour
into a freezing tray or plastic tray and leave in the ice-
making compartment of the refrigerator for 1 hour or until
frozen 1in at sides.
6 Remove mixture from refrigerator, scrape into chilled
mixer bowl and run machine until mixture is smooth. Return
to tray and re-freeze for 1 hour, or until firm. Turn refrigerator
back to normal setting.

NOTE: For a more economical recipe, use a small can of
evaporated milk instead of cream. Whisk until thick and
creamy, then fold into the cooled custard.
To vary the flavour:
Chocolate: Reduce sugar to 1 level tablespoon and stir 2oz
plain chocolate into custard before cooling.
Coffee: Omit vanilla essence and add 1 level tablespoon
instant coffee to custard powder before making custard.

1 4   MAYONNAISE (A)
(for mixers)

1 egg yolk
½ level teaspoon salt
¼ level teaspoon dry mustard
¼ level teaspoon castor sugar
½ pint salad oil
4 teaspoons vinegar or lemon juice
1 level tablespoon boiling water (optional)

1 Place egg yolk, salt, mustard and sugar in mixer bowl, or
in a basin; whisk until well mixed.
2 Add about 3 teaspoons oil, a drop at a time, whisking
well after each addition. Whisk in 1 teaspoon vinegar or
lemon juice.
3 Continue to add oil, a teaspoonful at a time, whisking
well after each addition. When mayonnaise thickens, whisk
in a teaspoonful of vinegar, and then continue adding oil
and vinegar until used up.
4 If a thinner, lighter mayonnaise is required, whisk in
boiling water when all the oil has been added.

2 5 6   MAYONNAISE (B)
(for liquidisers)

1 large egg
2 tablespoons vinegar
¼ level teaspoon salt
¼ level teaspoon dry mustard
Pinch of pepper
¼ level teaspoon sugar
½ pint corn oil
1 tablespoon boiling water

1 Place egg, vinegar, salt, mustard, pepper and sugar in
liquidiser goblet and run machine until mixed. Remove small
cap in lid and pour oil slowly into liquidiser in a steady
stream. Add boiling water and run machine until blended.
Store mayonnaise in an air-tight container in a cold place.
NOTE: If using a liquidiser without a small cap in the lid,
make a lid from a piece of foil to fit the top of liquidiser
goblet and pierce a small hole in centre. Pour the oil through
this hole. When using No. 6 type of liquidiser, double the
quantities of ingredients given above.

Baby Foods

You will find your liquidiser a great help when preparing foods for baby. Here are a few suggestions for baby foods, to show you how to use your machine. Check the instructions for your machine, as you may need to adapt the recipes to put gravy in with the meat. You'll find that, with the help of the liquidiser, baby's meals can be prepared using the same meat and desserts that you are preparing for the rest of the family.

2 5   BACON DINNER

2 rashers back bacon
1 rounded tablespoon mashed potato
1 rounded tablespoon cooked vegetables
2 tablespoons gravy

Lightly grill bacon; remove rind and excess fat, break into pieces and place in liquidiser goblet; run machine until bacon is roughly chopped. Add remaining ingredients; run machine until blended, adding more gravy, if necessary. Re-heat before serving.

LAMB AND TOMATO DINNER

1oz cooked lamb
2 tomatoes
2 tablespoons thick gravy
A pinch of sugar

1 Cut lamb into pieces and place in liquidiser goblet; run machine until finely chopped to suitable consistency for baby.
2 Place tomatoes in a basin and cover with boiling water; leave for 1 minute, drain. Peel tomatoes, cut in quarters and remove seeds.
3 Add tomato quarters to liquidiser goblet, with gravy and sugar; run machine until well blended with meat, and tomatoes are broken down. Heat before serving.

BEEF DINNER

1 rounded tablespoon cooked peas
2 tablespoons stock or water
1oz cooked beef
1 rounded tablespoon mashed potato
Gravy

1 Place peas and stock in liquidiser goblet and run machine until peas are well broken down; strain into a cup or small dish.
2 Cut beef in pieces and place in liquidiser goblet; run machine until meat is chopped to suitable consistency for baby. Add potatoes, and blend.
3 Add potato and beef mixture to peas, stir to mix and add sufficient gravy to suit child. Re-heat before serving.
NOTE: This recipe is also suitable for use with liver.

CHICKEN AND RICE DINNER

1oz cooked chicken
1 level tablespoon cooked rice
2 level tablespoons gravy or stock

1 Cut chicken into pieces and place in liquidiser goblet; run machine until chicken is chopped to suitable consistency for baby.
2 Add rice and gravy or stock; blend well, adding more gravy, if necessary.
NOTE: A little cooked vegetable can be added, if available.

APRICOT CUSTARD

2 tablespoons custard
6 canned or stewed apricot halves

Place both ingredients in liquidiser goblet and run machine until blended. Heat before serving, if desired.

FRUIT DESSERT

3 canned or stewed apricot halves
1 tablespoon cooked stewed apple
3 tablespoons apricot syrup or boiled water
2 rounded teaspoons baby cereal
1 rounded teaspoon honey (or to taste)

Place all ingredients in liquidiser goblet and run machine until well mixed. Heat before serving, if desired.

APPLE CUSTARD

2 tablespoons custard
2 tablespoons stewed apples

Place both ingredients in liquidiser goblet and run machine until well blended. Heat before serving, if desired.

BANANA DESSERT

5 tablespoons milk
1 level tablespoon semolina
1 teaspoon honey (or to taste)
1 small banana

Heat milk in a small saucepan and stir in semolina; bring to boil, stirring, and cook for 2 or 3 minutes. Add honey. Place in liquidiser goblet with banana, broken into rough pieces, and run machine until well blended. Heat before serving, if desired.

PINEAPPLE RICE

2 canned pineapple rings
2 tablespoons creamed rice or rice pudding

Break pineapple into rough pieces, place in liquidiser goblet, with rice; run machine until blended, and pineapple is of suitable consistency for baby. Heat before serving, if desired.

Starters and Snacks

Fluffy Cottage Eggs
An electric whisk will easily make this light, but satisfying dish. Besides being delicious, it is non-fattening

Quickly-made, first-course dishes and snacks can be prepared in your mixer and liquidiser. For delicious smooth soups, use fresh or canned vegetables or left-over vegetables and stock, made up from stock cubes. Smooth sauces and batters are prepared in a jiffy, too.

1 3 4 FLUFFY COTTAGE EGGS
(pictured left)

For 4 portions:
4 standard eggs
4oz cooked ham
8oz cottage cheese
½ level teaspoon salt
Black pepper
1 large (9oz) carton sliced green beans

1 Prepare a moderate oven (375 deg F, Gas Mark 5). Lightly grease 4 individual ovenproof dishes.
2 Separate eggs and place whites in mixer bowl (clean and grease free); place yolks in a basin. Chop ham.
3 Add cheese, ham and seasonings to yolks and mix well.
4 Whisk egg whites until stiff, but not dry. Switch off machine and fold in egg, cheese and ham mixture, using a metal spoon. Divide mixture between the 4 dishes.
5 Bake in centre of oven for 15 minutes, until fluffy and golden brown. Cook beans, following directions on carton.
6 To serve: Arrange beans around edges of dishes and serve immediately.

2 5 6 EGG AND ANCHOVY CROQUETTES

For 3 portions:
4 large eggs
½ pint milk
1½oz plain flour
1½ level tablespoons anchovy essence
Pepper
1½oz margarine
3oz fresh white breadcrumbs
Oil or lard for deep frying

1 Hard boil 3 eggs for 12 minutes; crack and leave in cold water to cool. Shell and dry on kitchen paper; chop roughly.
2 Place milk, flour and anchovy essence in liquidiser goblet, season with pepper, then run machine until blended.
3 Melt margarine in a small saucepan. Add contents of liquidiser goblet and stir over moderate heat until sauce comes to boil; simmer, stirring, for 2 minutes. Remove from heat, stir in chopped eggs, then turn on to a plate and leave to cool, stirring mixture occasionally, to prevent a skin forming.
4 When cold, cut into 6 on plate; shape each piece on a floured board into a croquette shape.
5 Beat remaining egg. Brush each croquette with egg, then roll in breadcrumbs; repeat coating once more.
6 Heat oil to 370 deg F, or until a 1in cube of day-old bread browns in 40 seconds. Fry croquettes until golden brown. Drain on kitchen paper. Serve hot.

2 5 SMOKED HADDOCK PATE

For 3 to 4 portions:
2 standard eggs
1 (8oz) carton frozen smoked haddock fillets
2oz butter, melted
8 tablespoons milk
Salt and pepper
Chopped parsley

1 Hard boil eggs for 10 minutes; drain, crack and leave in cold water to cool. Shell and dry on kitchen paper.
2 Cook haddock fillets as directed on carton. Remove fillets from bag and pour juices into liquidiser goblet. Remove any skin and bones from haddock, then chop fish roughly and place in goblet.
3 Add butter and milk, and season to taste. Run machine for a few seconds, to mix. Roughly chop eggs, add to liquidiser and run machine until pâté is smooth.
4 Turn pâté into a small serving dish and leave to chill. Serve, sprinkled with chopped parsley, with toast or Melba toast.

2 5 6 SPAGHETTI CHEESE

For 4 portions:
8oz quick-cooking spaghetti
3 large tomatoes
6oz Cheddar cheese
2oz plain flour
1 pint milk
Salt and pepper
2oz butter or margarine
1oz fresh white breadcrumbs

1 Cook spaghetti in a large saucepan of boiling, salted water for 7 minutes; drain and rinse with hot water. Place tomatoes in a bowl, cover with boiling water; leave for 1 minute, drain and skin.
2 Prepare a hot grill. Cut 5oz of cheese into ¾in cubes. Place cheese, flour and about one-third of milk in liquidiser goblet. Season with salt and pepper, and run machine until cheese is broken down.
3 Melt butter in a saucepan, add contents of liquidiser goblet and remaining milk; stir over moderate heat until sauce comes to boil. Simmer, stirring, for 2 minutes. Stir in spaghetti.
4 Pour into a shallow, 2-pint ovenproof dish. Slice tomatoes thinly and arrange on top of spaghetti. Grate remaining cheese and mix with breadcrumbs. Sprinkle over tomatoes; grill until topping is golden brown. Serve immediately.

1 3 4   COTTAGE CHEESE STRAWS

Makes 72:
10oz plain flour
1 level teaspoon salt
$\frac{1}{4}$ level teaspoon pepper
$\frac{1}{2}$ level teaspoon dry mustard
$\frac{1}{4}$ level teaspoon Cayenne pepper
2oz margarine
2oz lard
4oz cottage cheese
4oz Cheddar cheese, grated
Cold water

1 Prepare a hot oven (450 deg F, Gas Mark 8). Sift flour, salt, pepper, dry mustard and Cayenne pepper into mixer bowl. Add margarine and lard, cut into pieces. Switch on mixer at low speed and run machine until mixture resembles fine breadcrumbs.
2 Add cottage and grated cheese and run machine until well mixed.
3 Add about 4 tablespoons of water and mix with a fork to make a stiff dough; turn out on to a floured board. Roll out to a 12in square, then cut into $\frac{1}{2}$in strips. Cut each strip at 4in intervals to make 3 straws.
4 Place cheese straws on 2 baking sheets and bake in centre of oven until slightly risen and golden brown, for about 12 to 15 minutes. Leave to cool on baking sheet. Serve warm or cold.

1 3 4   POTATO SCONES

Makes 9:
4oz self-raising flour
1 level teaspoon baking powder
1 level teaspoon salt
$1\frac{1}{2}$oz margarine
6oz cold cooked potato
1 tablespoon milk

1 Sift flour, baking powder and salt into mixer bowl; add margarine, cut into pieces, and potato.
2 Switch on mixer at low speed and run machine until well mixed. Add milk and mix with a fork to form a dough.
3 Lightly grease a thick-based frying pan; place over moderate heat.
4 Roll out dough on a floured board to $\frac{1}{4}$in thickness. Cut into rounds with a $2\frac{1}{2}$in plain cutter. Arrange scones in frying pan and cook for 3 to 4 minutes, until golden brown; turn and cook on other side.
5 Serve scones hot, split and buttered.

2 5   STUFFED TOMATOES
(pictured on back cover)

For 3 portions:
6 large tomatoes
1 ($4\frac{1}{2}$oz) can sardines
2 rounded tablespoons fresh white breadcrumbs
Salt and pepper

1 Cut a thin slice from rounded end of each tomato. Scoop out seeds and tomato pulp with a teaspoon and place in liquidiser goblet.
2 Add contents of can of sardines to liquidiser goblet and run machine until well blended; turn into a bowl.
3 Add breadcrumbs and mix well. Season to taste. Pile into tomato shells and replace 'lids'. Serve with a green salad.

2 5 6   ZHIVAGO PASTIES

Makes 6:
8oz smoked haddock fillet
$\frac{1}{2}$ pint milk
1oz plain flour
1oz margarine
1 small (5oz) can garden peas
Salt and pepper
1 small egg
1 ($7\frac{1}{2}$oz) packet frozen puff pastry, just thawed

1 Prepare a hot oven (450 deg F, Gas Mark 8).
2 Wash haddock and place in a saucepan with milk; bring to boil, then simmer until haddock is cooked, about 8 to 10 minutes. Strain milk into liquidiser goblet.
3 Remove skin and any bones from haddock.
4 Add flour to milk and run machine until blended; add fish and run machine until just chopped.
5 Melt margarine in a saucepan, add contents of liquidiser goblet and stir over moderate heat until sauce comes to boil. Simmer, stirring, for 2 minutes. Drain and add peas; season to taste. Beat egg.
6 Roll out pastry on a floured board to an oblong, 12in by 8in. Trim edges, then cut into 6 (4in) squares.
7 Divide fish mixture between squares, brush edges of each square with beaten egg and fold corners to centre, over fish filling, to form an 'envelope'. Seal edges together firmly. Brush pasties with beaten egg and place on a baking sheet. Bake in centre of oven for 15 to 20 minutes, until golden brown. Serve hot.

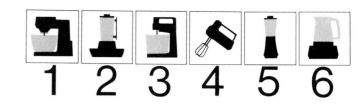

1 2 3 4 5 6

2 6   CHICKEN AND HAM PATE

For 6 to 8 portions:
SAVOURY WHITE SAUCE
1 small onion
½ pint milk
¼ level teaspoon celery salt
1 clove
Pinch of nutmeg
Salt and pepper
1oz plain flour
1oz margarine

6oz cooked chicken meat
6oz cooked lean ham
Large sprig of parsley
½ level teaspoon made mustard
Few drops of Worcester sauce

1 Peel onion and cut into quarters. Place milk, onion, celery salt, clove, nutmeg and seasonings in a small saucepan. Bring to boil, cover and leave in a warm place to infuse for about 15 minutes. Strain into liquidiser goblet.
2 Add flour to milk mixture and run machine until well blended. Melt margarine in a small saucepan. Add contents of liquidiser goblet and stir over moderate heat until sauce comes to boil; simmer, stirring, for 2 minutes.
3 Roughly chop chicken and ham.
4 Place sauce in liquidiser and switch to low speed. Gradually add chicken and ham; when well blended, add sprig of parsley, mustard and Worcester sauce. Turn to maximum speed until mixture is smooth.
5 Turn pâté into a serving dish and leave in a cool place to set. Serve with crisp toast.

---

2 5   COTTAGE CHEESE SLICE

For 4 portions:
1 medium-sized onion
1oz butter
2 standard eggs
2oz Cheddar cheese
1 (4oz) carton cottage cheese
Salt and pepper
1 (7½oz) packet frozen puff pastry, just thawed

1 Prepare a hot oven (450 deg F, Gas Mark 8). Rinse a baking sheet with cold water.
2 Peel and roughly chop onion. Melt butter in a small saucepan, add onion and cook gently until onion is soft, but not browned.
3 Separate 1 egg, place the white in liquidiser goblet and

yolk in small basin. Cut Cheddar cheese into ¾in cubes; add to liquidiser with remaining egg, cottage cheese, onion and butter, and a little seasoning. Run machine until mixture is smooth.
4 Roll out pastry on a floured board to a 12in square; trim edges and place on baking sheet. Pour cottage cheese mixture on to one half of pastry, leaving a 1in border around edge. Brush border with remaining egg yolk. Fold over pastry and seal edges together firmly.
5 Brush pastry with egg yolk, then make 6 slits, 2in long, at 2in intervals along top of slice, through one layer of pastry.
6 Bake in centre of oven for 15 to 20 minutes until risen and golden brown. Serve warm, cut into slices.

---

2 5 6   SEAFOOD PANCAKES

For 4 portions:
Half a green pepper
1oz margarine
1oz plain flour
½ pint milk
1 small (5oz) can peeled prawns
1 small (3⅞oz) can crab meat
Salt and pepper

PANCAKES
4oz plain flour
¼ level teaspoon salt
1 standard egg
½ pint milk
Lard for frying

1 Remove seeds and white pith from green pepper and cut into strips. Melt margarine in a small saucepan; add green pepper, cover, and cook slowly for 4 minutes.
2 Place flour and milk in liquidiser goblet and run machine until well mixed. Add to saucepan and bring to boil, stirring; cook for 3 minutes. Drain and rinse prawns, flake crab meat and add to sauce; season to taste.
3 Prepare pancakes: Place flour, salt, egg and milk into liquidiser goblet and run machine until blended.
4 Heat a little lard in a medium-sized frying pan. Pour off any excess lard into a small bowl, leaving pan lightly greased. Pour sufficient batter into pan, swirling quickly to coat pan thinly; cook until underside is golden brown.
5 Slip pancake to side of pan opposite handle, and quickly toss (or flip over with a palette knife); cook over moderate heat until brown. Slip on to a plate, place a portion of sauce on pancake and roll up. Make 8 pancakes in all and fill.
6 Place on a warm serving dish and garnish with peas or tomatoes.

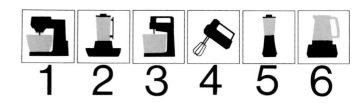

2 5 6 FLORENTINE SUPPER DISH

For 3 portions:
3 standard eggs
1 (8oz) carton frozen spinach
4oz Cheddar cheese
1oz plain flour
½ pint milk
Salt and pepper
1oz butter or margarine

1 Hard boil eggs for 10 minutes; crack and leave in cold water to cool. Shell and dry on kitchen paper; cut into halves, lengthwise.
2 Cook spinach according to directions on carton. Prepare a hot grill.
3 Cut cheese into ¾in cubes. Place cheese, flour and milk in liquidiser goblet; season with salt and pepper, and run machine until cheese is broken down.
4 Melt butter in a small saucepan, add contents of liquidiser goblet and stir over a moderate heat until sauce comes to boil. Simmer, stirring, for 2 minutes.
5 Place spinach in a shallow ovenproof dish; arrange eggs on top and coat with sauce. Place under grill until golden brown. Serve immediately.

---

2 5 6 CHEESE PUFF

For 3 portions:
3 slices white bread
3oz Cheddar cheese
¼ pint milk
1oz butter or margarine
2 standard eggs
Salt and pepper

1 Prepare a moderately hot oven (400 deg F, Gas Mark 6). Grease a 1½-pint pie dish.
2 Remove crusts and break bread into small pieces and place a little at a time in the liquidiser goblet, run machine until crumbed, then turn crumbs into a bowl. Cut cheese into ¾in dice and place in liquidiser.
3 Place milk and butter in a small saucepan and bring to boil. Separate eggs and place egg whites in a large, clean, grease-free bowl and egg yolks in liquidiser. Add milk and run machine until well blended. Pour on to breadcrumbs; season with salt and pepper.
4 Whisk egg whites until stiff, but not dry; fold into breadcrumb mixture. Turn into pie dish and bake in centre of oven for 25 to 30 minutes, until well risen and deep golden brown. Serve immediately.

2 5 6 SEAFOOD SCALLOPS
(pictured right)

For 6 portions:
1½lb potatoes
2oz margarine
Milk
Salt and pepper
1lb haddock fillet
Half a bay leaf
1 small onion
1oz plain flour
1 (4½oz) can peeled prawns or 4 oz fresh peeled prawns
½oz butter
1oz fresh white breadcrumbs
Parsley

1 Peel potatoes and cook in boiling, salted water; drain, dry over a low heat, and mash with 1oz margarine and a little milk. Season to taste.
2 Wash haddock, dry on kitchen paper and place in a saucepan with bay leaf. Measure ½ pint of milk and add to haddock. Peel, slice and add onion. Poach haddock for 8 to 10 minutes, depending on thickness; drain, reserving milk. Strain milk into liquidiser goblet. Flake haddock, discarding skin and any bones.
3 Add 1 level teaspoon salt, ½ level teaspoon pepper and flour to milk in liquidiser goblet; run machine until well mixed.
4 Melt remaining margarine in a saucepan, add milk mixture and stir over moderate heat until sauce thickens and comes to boil. Simmer, stirring continuously, for 2 minutes. Stir in flaked haddock.
5 Rinse prawns, if using canned ones, and add to haddock. Taste and adjust seasonings, if necessary.
6 Prepare a moderately hot oven (400 deg F, Gas Mark 6). Place potato in a piping bag fitted with a large star tube and pipe around edges of 6 deep scallop shells or individual dishes. Spoon fish mixture into centre of each shell. Melt butter in small saucepan, add breadcrumbs and stir until well mixed. Sprinkle over fish.
7 Place shells on a baking sheet and cook in centre of oven for 15 to 20 minutes, until potato is lightly browned. Garnish each shell with a sprig of parsley. Serve hot.
NOTE: Alternatively, brown potato under grill and breadcrumbs in pan, then divide fish mixture between shells and sprinkle with browned crumbs.

Seafood Scallops

An attractive starter for a special dinner party, these scallops can be made in advance and heated through in the oven. They would also make a tasty, light-luncheon or buffet-supper dish

2 5 6   CAULIFLOWER CHEESE

For 4 portions:
1 cauliflower
4oz cheese
1oz plain flour
$\frac{1}{2}$ pint milk
Salt and pepper
1oz butter or margarine

1 Trim tough outside leaves from cauliflower; hollow out thick lower part of stalk. Place in a large saucepan of boiling, salted water. Return to boil, cover and simmer for 20 to 25 minutes, until stalk and leaves are tender. Lift out of saucepan and drain carefully. Place in a serving dish and keep warm.
2 Cut cheese into $\frac{3}{4}$in cubes. Place cheese, flour and milk in liquidiser goblet. Season with salt and pepper and run machine until cheese is broken down.
3 Melt butter in a small saucepan, add contents of liquidiser goblet and stir over moderate heat until sauce comes to boil; simmer, stirring, for 2 minutes.
4 Pour sauce over cauliflower and serve immediately.

1 3 4   KIPPER-STUFFED POTATOES

For 4 portions:
4 large potatoes
1 small (7oz) can kipper fillets
2oz butter
2 standard eggs
3 tablespoons milk
$\frac{1}{2}$ level teaspoon salt
$\frac{1}{4}$ level teaspoon pepper

1 Prepare a moderate oven (350 deg F, Gas Mark 4).
2 Wash and scrub potatoes and remove eyes; prick all over with a fork.
3 Place potatoes in oven and bake until soft, for $1\frac{1}{4}$ to $1\frac{3}{4}$ hours, depending on size.
4 Drain oil from kipper fillets and remove skin; place in mixer bowl. Add butter, eggs, milk and seasonings.
5 When potatoes are cooked, remove from oven and increase oven temperature to hot (450 deg F, Gas Mark 8). Cut a thin slice from top of each potato and scoop out insides, leaving just enough to form a thin wall; add to mixer bowl.
6 Switch on mixer at low speed and mix until smooth;pile back into potato skins. Place potatoes on a baking sheet and return to oven for 15 to 20 minutes, until tops are golden brown. Serve hot.

1   CHEESY HAM CRESCENT

For 4 to 6 portions:
SCONE DOUGH
3oz Cheddar cheese
1oz cooked ham or bacon
8oz self-raising flour
1 level teaspoon baking powder
1 level teaspoon salt
$\frac{1}{4}$ level teaspoon dry mustard
2oz best-quality margarine
1 standard egg
7 tablespoons milk

GARNISH
Tomato wedges
Watercress

1 Prepare a hot oven (425 deg F, Gas Mark 7). Lightly grease a baking sheet. Grate cheese and chop ham or bacon.
2 Reserve a tablespoon of cheese and place all other scone ingredients (cut margarine into small pieces) in mixer bowl; mix at moderate speed until well blended.
3 Turn out on to a floured board and shape into a roll, about 8in long. Make 8 cuts, 1in apart, down one side of roll. Place on baking sheet and curve roll so that cut sides splay out. Brush with milk and sprinkle with remaining cheese.
4 Bake in centre of oven for 15 to 20 minutes, until risen and golden brown. Remove from baking sheet and cool slightly on a wire rack.
5 Serve either warm or cold, garnished with tomato wedges between cuts, and watercress.

2 5   SALMON PATE

For 2 to 3 portions:
1 small ($7\frac{1}{2}$oz) can red salmon
2 teaspoons anchovy essence
2 teaspoons lemon juice
1 small ($2\frac{7}{8}$ fluid oz) carton double cream
1oz fresh white breadcrumbs

1 Drain liquid from can of salmon into liquidiser goblet. Remove skin and large bones from salmon, then place fish in goblet with anchovy essence, lemon juice and cream. Run machine until mixture is smooth.
2 Pour mixture into a bowl, mix in breadcrumbs, then turn into a small serving dish and leave to chill until required. Serve pâté with toast or Melba toast and butter.

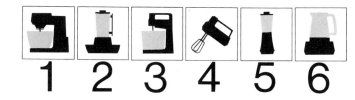

2 5   TUNA BURGERS

For 4 portions:
¼ pint milk
1oz plain flour
1 level tablespoon tomato ketchup
Salt and pepper
1 (7oz) can tuna steak
2oz margarine
1 standard egg
2oz fresh white breadcrumbs
4 baps or soft rolls

1 Place milk, flour and tomato ketchup in liquidiser goblet. Season with salt and pepper.
2 Add tuna to liquidiser; run machine until just blended.
3 Melt 1oz margarine in a small saucepan, add tuna mixture and stir over moderate heat until sauce comes to boil; cook, stirring, for 2 minutes. Turn out on to a plate and leave to cool.
4 Beat egg. Turn out tuna mixture on to a floured board, cut into 4 equal pieces; form each piece into a round patty. Coat with beaten egg, then with breadcrumbs.
5 Place baps in a cool oven to heat through. Melt remaining margarine in a frying pan, fry Tuna Burgers until golden brown on each side.
6 To serve: Cut baps in half, place a Tuna Burger on base of each roll and cover with other half. Serve immediately, with tomato or mushroom soup.

1 2 3 4 5
EGG AND BACON TARTLETS

Makes 12:
SHORTCRUST PASTRY
8oz plain flour
1 level teaspoon salt
2oz lard
2oz margarine
Cold water to mix

FILLING
2oz streaky bacon
1 medium-sized onion
½oz lard
4oz Cheddar cheese
¼ pint milk
1 standard egg
Salt and pepper

1 Prepare a moderate oven (375 deg F, Gas Mark 5). Make pastry as directed on page 7. Roll out pastry on floured board and line 12 tartlet tins.

2 Remove rind and bone from bacon and cut into small pieces. Peel and chop onion. Melt lard in a frying pan and fry onion and bacon for 3 minutes.
3 Cut cheese in ¾in cubes. Place milk and cheese in liquidiser goblet and run machine until cheese is broken down. Add egg and a little salt and pepper; run machine until blended.
4 Divide bacon and onion between tartlets, pour egg mixture on top and cook until risen and golden brown, about 30 minutes. Serve hot or cold.

1 2 3 4 5 6
KENTUCKY FLAN

For 4 to 6 portions:
SHORTCRUST PASTRY
4oz plain flour
¼ level teaspoon salt
1oz margarine
1oz lard or cooking fat
Cold water to mix

FILLING
1oz plain flour
½ level teaspoon dry mustard
½ pint milk
1oz margarine
1 small (7oz) can sweet corn with peppers
¼lb lean ham, cut in strips
Salt and pepper
2 hard-boiled eggs

A little watercress

1 Prepare a hot oven (425 deg F, Gas Mark 7).
2 Make shortcrust pastry according to directions on page 7.
3 Roll out pastry and line a shallow 7in square tin, prick well and place a square of greaseproof paper in the bottom. Fill with baking beans or rice and bake in centre of oven for 15 minutes. Remove beans (or rice) and paper and cook for a further 5 minutes.
4 Place flour, mustard and milk in liquidiser goblet. Run machine until blended.
5 Melt margarine in a saucepan. Add milk mixture and stir over moderate heat until sauce boils. Simmer, stirring, for 2 minutes. Add contents of can of corn, ham and seasonings.
6 Prepare a moderate grill.
7 Slice eggs and lay over base of flan. Pour over sauce.
8 Re-heat under a moderate grill.
9 Place on a serving dish and decorate with sprigs of watercress. Serve hot.

Pork and Liver Pâté

This savoury pâté is perfect with salad and Melba toast. It would be equally good for a picnic lunch

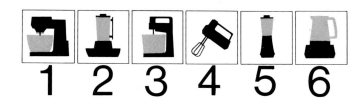

2 5 6 PORK AND LIVER PATE
(pictured left and on back cover)

For 8 portions:
6 rashers streaky bacon
1 large slice white bread
½lb lambs' liver
½lb belly pork
1½oz butter
1 level dessertspoon plain flour
Scant ½ pint milk
1 level teaspoon anchovy essence or salt
1 tablespoon single cream (optional)
Pepper

1 Prepare a moderate oven (350 deg F, Gas Mark 4).
2 Remove rind and bone from bacon and press rashers flat with a knife. Line base and sides of a 1lb loaf tin with rashers and press in firmly.
3 Break bread into pieces, place in liquidiser goblet and run machine until bread is reduced to fine crumbs; place in a bowl.
4 Remove any gristle from liver and cut into pieces. Remove rind and bone from pork and cut into small cubes.
5 Melt butter in a frying pan and gently fry liver and pork for 5 minutes. Remove from pan and place on a plate. Stir flour into fat remaining in pan. Add milk, anchovy essence (or salt), single cream (if used) and a shake of pepper. Bring to boil, stirring, and simmer for about 1 minute.
6 Place half the sauce and half the meat in liquidiser goblet and run machine until meat is broken down and blended with sauce; pour into bowl with breadcrumbs. Place remainder of sauce and meat in liquidiser and repeat; add to bowl and mix well. (If using one of the large types of machine, all the meat and sauce may be placed in machine at the same time.)
7 Pour into prepared tin; place tin in a larger tin containing about ½in depth of water and cook for 1½ hours. Leave to cool in tin, then turn out carefully and place on a serving dish or board. Garnish with watercress and serve with hot toast and butter.
NOTE: This pâté can also be served as a main meal.

2 CRISPY TOPPED TOMATOES

For 4 portions:
1 large (16oz) can peeled tomatoes
4oz Cheddar cheese
2 (1oz) packets potato crisps
Salt and pepper

1 Prepare a moderate oven (375 deg F, Gas Mark 5).
2 Turn contents of can of tomatoes into a 1½-pint ovenproof dish.

3 Cut cheese into ¾in dice. Place half the cheese and contents of 1 packet of crisps in liquidiser goblet and run machine until cheese and crisps are broken down; turn into a bowl. Repeat with remaining cheese and crisps.
4 Season cheese and crisps with a little salt and pepper, then sprinkle over tomatoes.
5 Place on a baking sheet and bake in the centre of oven for 30 minutes. Serve with grilled bacon, sausages or beefburgers.

2 5 BROCCOLI WITH HOLLANDAISE SAUCE

For 4 portions:
1 large (9oz) carton frozen broccoli spears
Hollandaise Sauce (see recipe on page 83)

1 Place broccoli in a large saucepan containing about ½in of boiling, salted water.
2 Bring back to boil, then reduce heat and simmer for 8 to 10 minutes, until broccoli is just tender.
3 Strain carefully. Return broccoli to saucepan and dry over a low heat for a few minutes. Lift carefully on to a dish and serve immediately with Hollandaise Sauce.

2 5 HADARONI

For 4 portions:
1lb smoked haddock
½ pint milk and water, mixed
Milk
6oz quick-cooking macaroni
2 hard-boiled eggs
1oz plain flour
1½oz butter
1 level dessertspoon chopped parsley
Lemon wedges

1 Wash and trim haddock; cut into even-sized pieces. Place fish, with mixed milk and water, in a saucepan. Bring to boil; cover and simmer for about 7 minutes, until fish is tender.
2 Remove fish from pan, reserving liquid. Remove any bones, then flake fish. Make liquid up to ¾ pint with milk.
3 Cook macaroni in boiling, salted water for 7 minutes; drain and rinse with hot water. Shell and chop eggs.
4 Place liquid from fish, and flour, in liquidiser goblet and run machine until well blended. Melt butter in a saucepan, add contents of goblet and stir over a moderate heat until sauce boils. Simmer, stirring, for 2 minutes.
5 Add fish, macaroni and eggs to sauce; mix well and turn into a warm serving dish.
6 Sprinkle with chopped parsley and garnish with lemon wedges. Serve immediately.

1 2 3 4 5
SAUSAGE CARTWHEEL FLAN

For 4 portions:
CHEESE PASTRY
4oz plain flour
Pinch of salt
1oz margarine
1oz lard
2oz Cheddar cheese, grated
Cold water to mix

FILLING
1 small onion
½oz lard
½lb skinless pork sausages
1 standard egg
7 tablespoons milk
Salt and pepper
1oz Cheddar cheese, grated

1 Prepare a moderately hot oven (375 deg F, Gas Mark 5).
2 Place flour and salt in mixer bowl, add fats,
cut into small pieces; and run machine until mixture
resembles fine breadcrumbs. Stir in cheese. Mix to a firm
dough with a little cold water. Roll out pastry and line a 7in
flan ring or sponge tin.
3 Peel and finely chop onion. Melt lard in a frying pan and
fry sausages until golden on all sides; remove from pan.
Fry onion until soft but not brown. Cut a ½in slice from one
end of each of 6 sausages. Place pieces, with the 2 whole
sausages, in liquidiser goblet. Place onion in flan case.
Arrange remaining 6 sausages radiating from centre of flan.
4 Add egg and milk to liquidiser, season, and run machine
until well blended and sausages are chopped. Pour into flan
case. Sprinkle cheese over flan.
5 Bake in the centre of oven for 40 minutes. Serve either
hot with baked tomatoes, or cold with salad.

2 5
JIFFY TOASTS

For 4 portions:
4 large slices bread
Butter
1 small (7oz) can luncheon meat
1 standard egg
¼ level teaspoon dry mustard
2 teaspoons Worcester sauce
1 level tablespoon tomato ketchup
Salt and pepper

1 Prepare a moderate grill. Toast bread on both sides, butter
and keep hot.
2 Cut luncheon meat into ½in dice.

3 Place luncheon meat, egg, mustard, Worcester sauce,
ketchup and seasonings in liquidiser goblet, and run
machine until luncheon meat has broken down.
4 Spread meat mixture on toast and place under grill until
lightly browned and bubbling. Serve immediately.

2 5
CHEESY SCRAMBLED EGGS

For 4 portions:
4oz Cheddar cheese
4 standard eggs
Salt and pepper
1oz butter
4 slices buttered toast
Paprika

1 Cut cheese into ¾in dice. Place in liquidiser goblet with
eggs and seasonings and run machine until cheese
is broken down.
2 Melt butter in a small saucepan. Add egg mixture and
cook over a low heat, stirring continuously with a wooden
spoon, until eggs are scrambled.
3 Pile on to toast, sprinkle with paprika and
serve immediately.

2 5
HAM AND PORK FRITTERS

For 4 portions:
1 standard egg
¼ pint milk
½ level teaspoon salt
Shake of pepper
½ level teaspoon mixed dried herbs
4oz self-raising flour
1 small (7oz) can chopped ham with pork
2oz lard

1 Break egg into liquidiser goblet. Add milk, salt, pepper
and mixed dried herbs and run machine until well blended.
Switch off machine, add flour, then run machine
until well blended.
2 Cut chopped ham with pork into small cubes and put in
a basin. Add batter from liquidiser and mix well.
3 Heat lard in a large frying pan and drop mixture in pan in
tablespoonsful. Cook over moderate heat for about 5
minutes, turning fritters when browned. Drain
on kitchen paper.
4 Serve immediately with baked beans or
fried tomato halves.

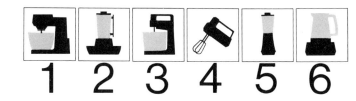

2 5 ASPARAGUS WITH HOLLANDAISE SAUCE

For 4 portions:
1lb fresh asparagus
Salt
Hollandaise Sauce (see recipe on page 83)

1 Scrape asparagus ends with a knife to remove tough skin.
Place tips together and trim ends to an even length.
Tie with string.
2 Pour sufficient water in a large, deep saucepan to cover
lower two thirds of asparagus. Add salt and bring to boil.
Gently place asparagus in water, propped against side of
saucepan, with lower ends immersed, but tips above water.
3 Return to boil, cover and simmer for 15 to 25 minutes,
depending on age of asparagus. When tips are tender,
remove bundle from water and drain well on kitchen paper.
4 Lift carefully on to a dish and serve immediately
with Hollandaise Sauce.

---

2 5 6 SALMON AND PRAWN SHELLS

For 4 portions:
1 small (7½oz) can pink salmon
½ pint fresh prawns
1 small (5oz) carton frozen peas
6oz shell pasta
Knob of butter

SAUCE
1oz plain flour
½ pint milk
1 level teaspoon tomato purée (optional)
1oz butter or margarine
Salt and pepper

Lemon twists
Parsley

1 Remove skin and bones from salmon and flake. Reserve
4 prawns and peel remainder. Cook peas, following
directions on carton.
2 Cook pasta shells in boiling, salted water for 13 to 15
minutes, or until tender. Drain and rinse with hot water.
Melt knob of butter in saucepan, return shells to pan and
toss until coated.
3 Make sauce: Place flour, milk and tomato purée (if used),
in liquidiser goblet and run machine until well blended. Melt
butter in a saucepan, add milk mixture and seasonings,
and cook over a moderate heat until sauce boils. Simmer,
stirring, for 2 minutes.

4 Add salmon, peeled prawns and peas. Spoon sauce into
4 large scallop shells or individual dishes. Arrange pasta
shells around edges to form a border.
5 To serve: Place scallop shells on a round plate, arrange a
lemon twist on each scallop shell and garnish
with parsley and a prawn.

---

2 5 CHOPPED PORK WITH CORN FRITTERS

For 4 portions:
1 small (7oz) can chopped pork
1 large (11oz) can sweet corn
Water
1 standard egg
4oz plain flour
Salt and pepper
Fat for frying

1 Cut chopped pork into 4 slices.
2 Drain sweet corn and make liquor up to ¼ pint with water.
3 Place liquor, egg, flour and seasonings in liquidiser goblet;
run machine until well blended, then stir in sweet corn.
4 Melt a little fat in a frying pan and drop tablespoonsful of
batter into frying pan. Fry until golden brown on each side.
Drain on kitchen paper and keep warm.
5 Fry slices of chopped pork lightly on each side, then serve
immediately with corn fritters.

---

1 3 4 BACON AND SWEET CORN PUFF

For 4 portions:
1 small (7oz) can sweet corn
4 rashers streaky bacon
2 tomatoes
1oz butter
4 standard eggs
2 tablespoons water
Salt and pepper

1 Drain sweet corn. Remove rind and bone from bacon and
cut into strips. Slice tomatoes.
2 Melt butter in an 8in or 9in frying pan. Add bacon and
sweet corn and cook for 2 to 3 minutes.
3 Remove rack from grill pan and prepare a moderate grill.
4 Separate eggs and place whites in mixer bowl (clean and
grease free). Beat yolks, water and seasonings together.
Whisk egg whites until stiff and carefully fold into egg yolk
mixture. Fold mixture into bacon and sweet corn in pan.
Cook slowly until sides have just set and
underside has browned.
5 Cover with slices of tomato and place under grill for 2
to 3 minutes, until risen and lightly browned.
6 Cut into 4 portions and serve immediately.

2 5 6 KIDNEY SOUP

For 4 portions:
1 medium-sized onion
4 lambs' kidneys
1oz margarine
1 pint water
1 level dessertspoon cornflour
¼ pint milk
Salt and pepper
Gravy browning (optional)
A little cream
Chopped parsley

1 Peel and slice onion. Remove skin and core from kidneys and cut into small pieces.
2 Melt margarine in a saucepan. Add onion and cook for 2 to 3 minutes. Add kidney to saucepan and cook for a further 4 minutes.
3 Add water, bring to boil, cover and simmer for 10 minutes.
4 Place cornflour in liquidiser goblet and add soup. Run machine until smooth. (Do not overfill liquidiser; divide soup into 2 or more batches.) Rinse saucepan. Pour soup through a strainer into saucepan.
5 Add milk and bring to boil; cook for 1 minute. Season to taste, and colour with a little gravy browning, if desired.
6 Serve with a spoonful of cream and a little chopped parsley on top of each bowl.

2 5 6 POTATO AND CELERY SOUP

For 4 portions:
1lb potatoes
4 or 5 sticks of celery
1¼ pints water
1 chicken stock cube
Salt and pepper
½ pint milk

1 Wash, peel and roughly dice potatoes. Wash celery and cut into short lengths.
2 Place vegetables in a saucepan with water, stock cube and seasonings. Bring to boil, stirring; cover and simmer for 20 minutes.
3 Place soup in liquidiser goblet and run machine until smooth. (Do not overfill liquidiser; divide soup into 2 or more batches.) Rinse saucepan.
4 Strain soup into saucepan; add milk, and season again, if necessary. Re-heat soup and serve piping hot.

2 5 6 LEEK AND POTATO SOUP
(pictured right)

For 6 portions:
1lb potatoes
1lb leeks
1 onion
2oz margarine
Salt and pepper
1¼ pints water
1 chicken stock cube
½ pint milk

1 Wash, peel and roughly dice potatoes. Thoroughly wash and trim leeks and cut in slices. Peel and slice onion.
2 Melt margarine in a saucepan, add vegetables, cover and cook gently for 5 minutes. Add a little seasoning, water and stock cube; bring to boil, cover and simmer for 20 minutes.
3 Place soup in liquidiser goblet and run machine until smooth. (Do not overfill liquidiser; divide soup into 2 or more batches.) Rinse saucepan.
4 Return soup to saucepan; add milk, season again, if necessary. Re-heat soup and serve piping hot with fried bread cubes.

2 5 6 SWEET CORN SOUP
(pictured on back cover)

For 4 to 6 portions:
1 medium-sized onion
1 large potato
2oz margarine
1 chicken stock cube
2 level teaspoons salt
Pepper
1½ pints water
1 large (11oz) can sweet corn kernels
¼ pint milk
2 level teaspoons cornflour

1 Peel and roughly chop onion and potato.
2 Melt margarine in a saucepan and fry onion and potato for 5 minutes. Add chicken stock cube, salt, pepper and water; bring to boil and simmer for 20 minutes.
3 Add contents of can of sweet corn; place in liquidiser goblet and run machine until smooth. (Do not overfill liquidiser; divide soup into 2 or more batches.) Rinse saucepan.
4 Strain soup back into saucepan. Blend milk into cornflour and add to soup, stirring. Bring to boil and cook for 3 minutes, stirring continuously.
5 Serve soup piping hot with triangles of toast.

2 5 6   CREAM OF CAULIFLOWER SOUP

For 5 portions:
1 medium-sized cauliflower
1 medium-sized onion
1½oz margarine
1 pint water
1 level teaspoon salt
¼ level teaspoon pepper
¼ level teaspoon ground nutmeg
½ pint milk
1oz plain flour

1 Wash cauliflower and cut into sprigs, discarding tough outside leaves. Peel and roughly chop onion.
2 Melt margarine in a large saucepan. Add cauliflower and onion, and fry over a moderate heat for 2 minutes, without browning. Add water and salt and pepper. Bring to boil, cover and simmer for 20 to 25 minutes, until cauliflower is soft.
3 Place soup in liquidiser goblet and run machine until smooth. (Do not overfill liquidiser; divide soup into 2 or more batches.) Rinse saucepan.
4 Return soup to saucepan and add nutmeg.
5 Place milk and flour in liquidiser goblet and run machine until well mixed; add to soup. Stir over a moderate heat until soup thickens and comes to boil; simmer for 3 minutes, stirring continuously. Taste and adjust seasonings, if necessary. Serve piping hot.
NOTE: When cauliflowers are expensive, use half a cauliflower and add 1 peeled, chopped potato and a chicken stock cube.

2 5 6   HAM AND PEA SOUP

For 4 portions:
1 chicken stock cube
¾ pint boiling water
1 large (10½oz) can garden peas
2 slices of cooked ham
¼ pint milk
Salt and pepper

1 Dissolve stock cube in boiling water. Add contents of can of peas and 1 slice of ham.
2 Place soup in liquidiser goblet and run machine until blended. (Do not overfill liquidiser; divide soup into 2 or more batches.) Place in a saucepan.
3 Add milk to saucepan and bring slowly to boil, stirring; season to taste.
4 Cut remaining slice of ham in small dice.
5 Pour hot soup into a warm serving dish and sprinkle diced ham on top.

2 5 6   TOMATO AND CELERY SOUP

For 4 to 6 portions:
1lb tomatoes
1 large potato
2 sticks of celery
1 chicken stock cube
¾ pint water
½ pint milk or water
Salt and pepper

1 Wash and quarter tomatoes. Wash, peel and roughly chop potato. Wash and chop celery.
2 Place vegetables in a large saucepan with chicken stock cube and the water. Bring to boil, cover and simmer for 20 minutes.
3 Place soup in liquidiser goblet and run machine until smooth. (Do not overfill liquidiser; divide soup into 2 or more batches.) Rinse saucepan.
4 Strain liquid back into saucepan and add milk or water. Season, if necessary. Re-heat soup and serve piping hot, with fried bread cubes.

2 5 6   LENTIL AND BACON SOUP

For 6 portions:
1 bacon knuckle
2 carrots
1 large onion
8oz lentils
2 pints water
Salt and pepper
Chopped parsley

1 Soak bacon knuckle for a few hours or overnight.
2 Peel and roughly chop carrots and onion.
3 Place bacon knuckle, carrots, onion, lentils and water in a large saucepan. Bring to boil, cover and simmer for about 1 hour, until lentils are tender. Remove knuckle.
4 Place soup in liquidiser goblet and run machine until smooth. (Do not overfill liquidiser; divide soup into 2 or more batches.) Rinse saucepan.
5 Return soup to saucepan; taste and season. Re-heat soup, and serve piping hot, sprinkled with chopped parsley.
NOTE: If desired, soup may be diluted with a little milk. Alternatively, omit knuckle and water, and use 2 pints of bacon stock.

2 5 6   CREAM OF CUCUMBER SOUP

For 4 portions:
1 cucumber
1 chicken stock cube
$\frac{3}{4}$ pint water
$\frac{1}{4}$ pint milk
1 tablespoon single cream or top of the milk
Salt and pepper

1 Wash cucumber and trim, if necessary. Cut into thick slices, then into quarters. Place in a saucepan with chicken stock cube and water; bring to boil, cover and simmer for 5 minutes.
2 Place soup in liquidiser goblet and run machine until smooth. (Do not overfill liquidiser; divide soup into 2 or more batches.) Rinse saucepan.
3 Strain soup into saucepan, add milk and cream and bring to boil. Season to taste. Serve piping hot.

2 5 6   BEEF AND BEAN SOUP

For 6 portions:
1 large onion
1 medium-sized carrot
1 stick of celery (or 1 level teaspoon celery salt)
1oz margarine
4oz corned beef
1 small (8oz) can baked beans with tomato sauce
1$\frac{1}{2}$ pints water
2 beef extract cubes
Salt and pepper

1 Peel and slice onion and carrot; wash and slice celery.
2 Place margarine in a saucepan, add vegetables and fry, stirring occasionally, for 5 minutes. Cut up corned beef.
3 Add corned beef, baked beans and the water; crumble and add beef extract cubes. Bring to boil, cover and simmer for 20 minutes.
4 Place soup in liquidiser goblet and run machine until smooth. (Do not overfill liquidiser; divide soup into 2 or more batches.) Rinse saucepan.
5 Return soup to saucepan. Season, if necessary. Re-heat and serve piping hot.

2 5 6   WATERCRESS AND POTATO SOUP

For 4 to 6 portions:
1 bunch of watercress
1lb potatoes
2 pints water
1 chicken stock cube
2 level dessertspoons cornflour
Milk
Salt and pepper

1 Wash watercress; set aside a few sprigs for garnish. Peel and cube potatoes. Place in a saucepan with watercress, water and stock cube and bring to boil. Cover and simmer for 20 minutes.
2 Place soup in liquidiser goblet and run machine until smooth. (Do not overfill liquidiser; divide soup into 2 or more batches.) Rinse saucepan.
3 Return soup to saucepan. Blend cornflour with a little milk. Add to the purée and cook for 1 minute. Season to taste.
4 Serve in bowls, garnished with sprigs of watercress.
NOTE: To make a more substantial dish, serve with cubes of crisp, fried bread.

2 5   STUFFED MUSHROOMS

For 4 portions:
8 large mushrooms
2 rashers streaky bacon
$\frac{1}{2}$oz lard
2 standard eggs
2 tablespoons milk
Salt and pepper
Parsley
4 slices buttered toast

1 Wash mushrooms and remove stalks. Place stalks in liquidiser goblet. Remove rind and bone from bacon and cut into small pieces.
2 Melt lard in a frying pan and fry mushrooms lightly on both sides. Remove from pan and keep warm.
3 Add eggs and milk to mushroom stalks in liquidiser, add seasonings, and run machine until stalks are chopped.
4 Place bacon in a saucepan and fry until crisp; add egg mixture and cook until lightly scrambled.
5 Pile egg mixture on mushrooms and decorate each with a sprig of parsley. Serve on toast.

Herb Scone Ring
Serve these quickly-made savoury scones with cubes of cheese and tomatoes for a tasty supper snack

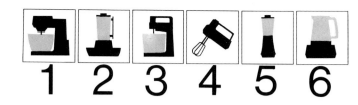

1 3 4   HERB SCONE RING
(pictured left)

Makes 12 scones:
8oz self-raising flour
1 rounded teaspoon salt
2oz margarine
1 level teaspoon mixed dried herbs
1 standard egg
Milk

1 Prepare a hot oven (425 deg F, Gas Mark 7). Grease an 8in sandwich tin.
2 Place flour and salt in mixer bowl. Add margarine, cut into small pieces, and run machine until mixture resembles fine breadcrumbs.
3 Stir in mixed herbs. Beat egg, add to mixture with about 5 tablespoonsful of milk and mix, with a fork, to a soft dough.
4 Turn out on to a floured board. Roll out to ½in thickness and cut into 12 rounds with a 2in cutter. Brush rounds with milk and arrange around inside edge of tin, slightly over-lapping.
5 Bake just above centre of oven for 15 to 20 minutes until risen and golden brown. Leave to cool in tin for a few minutes, then turn out on to a wire rack. Serve with butter, cubes of cheese and slices of tomato.

1 3 4   FRANKFURTER TWISTS

Makes 12:
2 small (8oz) cans frankfurter sausages
4 level tablespoons mixed pickle

CHEESE PASTRY
6oz plain flour
Salt and pepper
¼ level teaspoon dry mustard
3oz margarine
4oz Cheddar cheese
3 tablespoons cold water

1 Prepare a moderately hot oven (400 deg F, Gas Mark 6). Lightly grease a baking sheet.
2 Drain sausages; split each lengthwise and fill with pickle, using a teaspoon.
3 Place flour, a little salt and pepper and the mustard into mixer bowl. Add margarine, cut into small pieces, and run machine until mixture resembles fine breadcrumbs.
4 Grate cheese and mix in. Add the water and mix with a fork to form a firm dough.
5 Roll out pastry on a floured board and trim edges to make a 12in square.

6 Cut into 12 (1in) strips, and wrap each strip around a sausage. Place on greased baking sheet, with split sides of sausages uppermost, and bake for 15 to 20 minutes until pastry is golden brown. Serve hot or cold.

2 5 6   CAULIFLOWER SUISSE

For 3 portions:
1 large cauliflower

SAUCE
1oz plain flour
½ pint milk
1 medium-sized onion
1oz butter
1 (5 fluid oz) carton natural yoghourt
3 level teaspoons chopped parsley
Salt and pepper

1 Remove outer leaves from cauliflower and cut into sprigs. Cook in boiling, salted water for 12 minutes, or until tender; drain well and keep warm in a serving dish.
2 Place flour and milk in liquidiser goblet. Run machine until well blended.
3 Peel and chop onion. Melt butter in a saucepan and fry onion for 5 minutes or until tender, but not brown. Add milk mixture and stir over moderate heat until sauce boils. Simmer, stirring, for 2 minutes. Remove from heat.
4 Stir in yoghourt and parsley. Season to taste and pour over cauliflower sprigs.

1 2 4 5 6   SEAFOOD COCKTAIL

For 6 portions:
1 level tablespoon tomato ketchup
¼ pint mayonnaise (see either recipe on page 12)
1 small (3½oz) can peeled prawns
1 (7½oz) can crab meat
Lettuce
6 slices lemon

1 Stir ketchup into mayonnaise. Drain and rinse prawns, then dry on kitchen paper. Drain crab meat and remove any tendons.
2 Stir prawns and crab meat into mayonnaise.
3 Finely shred lettuce and place a little in the bottom of 6 glasses. Divide crab mixture and place on top of lettuce. Garnish each glass with a slice of lemon.

2 5 6
BROAD BEANS WITH SAVOURY SAUCE

For 4 portions:
2lb broad beans
2oz streaky bacon
2oz mushrooms
1oz plain flour
½ pint milk
1oz margarine
2 tablespoons single cream or top of the milk
Salt and pepper

1 Shell beans and cook in boiling, salted water until tender, about 10 to 20 minutes, depending on age of beans; drain.
2 Remove rind and bone from bacon and cut into thin strips. Wash and slice mushrooms.
3 Place flour and milk in liquidiser goblet and run machine until well blended.
4 Melt margarine in a small saucepan, add bacon and mushrooms and cook for 5 minutes. Add milk mixture and stir over moderate heat until sauce boils. Simmer, stirring, for 4 minutes.
5 Add single cream or top of the milk, beans, and season to taste; re-heat. Turn into a warm dish and serve.

2 5 6
CHEESY PASTA BOWS

For 4 portions:
4oz pasta bows
5oz Cheddar cheese
1 small (5oz) carton frozen peas
1oz plain flour
½ pint milk
Salt and pepper
1oz margarine
2oz cooked ham in one piece
2 small tomatoes

1 Cook pasta bows in boiling, salted water until tender, about 12 minutes. Drain and rinse thoroughly in hot water. Cut 4oz of the cheese into ¾in dice.
2 Cook peas, following directions on carton; drain.
3 Place diced cheese, flour, milk and seasonings in liquidiser goblet. Run machine until cheese is broken down. Melt margarine in a saucepan. Add milk mixture and stir over a moderate heat until sauce boils. Simmer, stirring, for 2 minutes.
4 Prepare a hot grill.
5 Cut ham into 1in dice, stir into sauce, with pasta and peas. Pour into a shallow 1½-pint ovenproof dish. Grate remaining cheese and sprinkle on top.

6 Cut tomatoes into slices, then halve slices and arrange around edges of dish. Cook under a hot grill until golden brown.

1 2 4 5 6 EGG MAYONNAISE

For 4 snack portions:
8 standard eggs
Lettuce
¼ pint mayonnaise (see either recipe on page 12)
Cayenne pepper
Watercress

1 Hard boil eggs for 10 minutes; crack and leave in cold water to cool. Shell and dry on kitchen paper.
2 Arrange a bed of lettuce on a serving dish. Cut eggs in halves lengthwise and place, cut sides downwards over the lettuce.
3 Spoon a little mayonnaise over each egg and sprinkle with Cayenne pepper. Garnish with sprigs of watercress.
NOTE: Serve only 1 egg per portion as an hors d'oeuvre.

2 6 SAVOURY CREAMED CAULIFLOWER

For 3 portions:
1 cauliflower

SAUCE
1½oz plain flour
½ pint milk
3 sprigs of parsley
Salt and pepper
4 rashers streaky bacon
1oz margarine

1 Wash cauliflower. Keep whole and remove thick stalk and coarse leaves. Cook in boiling, salted water until tender, about 15 to 20 minutes. Carefully lift out and drain. Place on a warm dish and keep hot. Keep ¼ pint of cauliflower stock.
2 Place flour, milk, cauliflower stock, parsley and seasonings in liquidiser goblet. Run machine until parsley is chopped.
3 Remove rind and bone from bacon, cut into strips and fry in small saucepan with margarine for 5 minutes. Add milk mixture and stir over moderate heat until sauce boils. Simmer, stirring, for 2 minutes.
4 Pour sauce over cauliflower, and serve immediately.
NOTE: Two chopped, hard-boiled eggs may be added to sauce before serving.

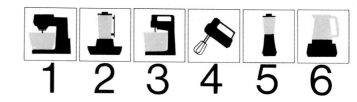

2 5 6 HAM AND CELERY MORNAY

For 4 portions:
1 large head of celery
Salt
4 slices cooked ham

CHEESE SAUCE
4oz cheese
1oz plain flour
$\frac{1}{4}$ pint milk
$\frac{1}{4}$ pint celery stock
$\frac{1}{2}$ level teaspoon made mustard
Pepper
1oz margarine

1 Trim celery, wash, and cut off coarse stalks; cut lengthwise into quarters. Place in a large saucepan, cover with salted water and bring to boil. Cover and simmer for 35 to 45 minutes until tender. Lift out carefully. Reserve stock for sauce, wrap a slice of ham around each piece of celery and place in a shallow, oblong ovenproof dish.
2 Prepare a medium grill.
3 Make sauce: Cut half the cheese into $\frac{3}{4}$in dice and grate remainder. Place diced cheese in liquidiser goblet with flour, milk, celery stock, mustard and pepper; run machine until cheese is broken down. Melt margarine in a saucepan, add contents of liquidiser goblet and stir over a moderate heat until sauce boils. Simmer, stirring, for 2 minutes. Taste and season, if necessary.
4 Pour sauce over celery rolls, sprinkle with remaining cheese, and grill until brown. Serve immediately.

1 3 4 SAUSAGE AND EGG FLUFFS

For 4 portions:
1 small onion
1lb pork sausagemeat
1 level tablespoon plain flour
$\frac{1}{2}$ level teaspoon salt
Pepper
$\frac{1}{2}$ level teaspoon dried sage
4 standard eggs

1 Peel and finely chop the onion.
2 Remove rack from grill pan and prepare a moderate grill.
3 Place onion, sausagemeat, flour, salt, pepper and sage in a bowl. Mix together until well blended.
4 Turn out on to a floured board and shape into 4 rounds.
5 Place in grill pan and grill for 15 minutes, turning once.

6 Separate eggs, put whites in mixer bowl (clean and grease free) and keep yolks in egg shells. Add a pinch of salt to egg whites and whisk until stiff.
7 Divide egg whites and pile on top of sausagemeat rounds; form into 'nests' with the back of a spoon. Carefully drop egg yolks into 'nests' and spoon over a little fat from grill pan.
8 Return to grill and cook for 2 to 3 minutes, until fluffy and golden brown. Serve immediately.

1 3 4 JACKETED EGGS

For 4 portions:
5 standard eggs
$\frac{1}{2}$lb streaky bacon
1$\frac{1}{2}$lb potatoes
1oz margarine
Salt and pepper
Plain flour
2 tablespoons water
4oz fresh white breadcrumbs
Cooking oil or fat for deep frying

1 Hard boil 4 eggs for 10 minutes; crack and leave in cold water to cool.
2 Remove rind and bone from bacon and cut into strips. Place in a small saucepan and fry until golden.
3 Peel potatoes and cook in boiling, salted water until tender; drain and dry over a low heat. Place in mixer bowl and run machine until potatoes are broken down. Add margarine, bacon and seasonings; mix well.
4 Remove shells from eggs and dust each one with a little flour. Mould a quarter of potato mixture around each egg, taking care to seal joins.
5 Beat together remaining egg and water on a saucer, and place breadcrumbs on a sheet of greaseproof paper. Place coated eggs singly in saucer, brush with beaten egg, then roll in breadcrumbs. Shake off excess crumbs and coat a second time with egg and crumbs. Shake off excess crumbs and re-shape.
6 Fill a deep-fat pan one third full with cooking oil or fat and heat to 370 deg F (when a small piece of day-old bread will brown in 40 seconds). Place coated eggs in a frying basket and fry steadily for about 5 minutes, until crisp and golden. Drain on crumpled kitchen paper and serve immediately.

Main Meals

Braised Stuffed Chicken
A savoury stuffing keeps a chicken moist and makes it go further. This chicken dish, with its accompanying vegetables, makes a hearty meal

Make exciting stuffings for roast joints and fish, as well as extra-light pastry, smooth sauces and batters, using a mixer or liquidiser. These recipes show you how main meals can be more varied and more quickly prepared.

2 6 BRAISED STUFFED CHICKEN
(pictured left)

For 4 to 6 portions:
1 frozen 3lb chicken, just thawed

STUFFING
1 small onion
3oz white bread, with crusts removed
1 sprig of parsley
1 small (7oz) can sweet corn
Salt and pepper
1 standard egg

1oz margarine
½lb small carrots
2 small leeks
1 small (4½oz) carton garden peas

1 Prepare a moderately hot oven (400 deg F, Gas Mark 6). Remove giblets from chicken and simmer in 1 pint of water, to make stock. Peel and cut onion into quarters.
2 Place onion, bread and parsley in liquidiser goblet and run machine until bread is crumbed and onion chopped; turn into a bowl.
3 Drain sweet corn and add 3 level tablespoonsful to the bowl, with seasonings. Lightly beat egg and add to stuffing; mix well. Stuff neck end of chicken and place remainder in body cavity. Truss chicken, if necessary.
4 Melt margarine in a frying pan and fry chicken for 5 minutes, turning occasionally, until browned.
5 Peel or scrape carrots and cut across into 1in lengths. Thoroughly wash and trim leeks and cut in 1in lengths; mix vegetables together and place in a large casserole.
6 Place chicken on top of vegetables, pour ½ pint of giblet stock over and season well; cover, and bake in centre of oven for 1 hour. Add peas and remaining corn, and cook for a further 5 minutes, or until tender.
7 Place chicken on a warm serving dish and spoon vegetables around.

1 2 3 6 SAVOURY CORNED BEEF ROLLS

For 5 portions:
1lb potatoes
1 onion
2oz margarine
1 large (12oz) can corned beef
1 small (5oz) can garden peas
Salt and pepper
10 rashers streaky bacon
Tomatoes

1 Prepare a moderately hot oven (400 deg F, Gas Mark 6).
2 Wash and peel potatoes. Cook in boiling, salted water until tender; drain and dry over low heat. Place in mixer bowl.
3 Peel and quarter onion and place in liquidiser goblet; run machine until roughly chopped. Melt margarine in a small saucepan; add onion and cook gently, covered, for 10 minutes or until soft but not brown.
4 Break corned beef into rough pieces. Drain peas. Add corned beef and onion to potato and run machine until mixed thoroughly. Add peas and mix in lightly; season to taste.
5 Remove rind and bone from bacon and spread each rasher flat with the back of a knife.
6 Shape corned beef mixture into 10 rolls and wrap each in a rasher. Place in an ovenproof dish. Bake in centre of oven for 10 minutes. Halve tomatoes, place around rolls and continue cooking for a further 10 minutes, until bacon is crisp and brown. Serve hot.

2 5 KROMESKIES

For 4 portions:
6oz to 8oz cooked chicken
¼ pint milk
1oz plain flour
1oz margarine
Salt and pepper
8 rashers back bacon

BATTER
¼ pint milk
1 standard egg
4oz plain flour
Salt

Fat for deep frying
Parsley to garnish

1 Cut chicken into small dice.
2 Place milk and flour in liquidiser goblet; run machine until well mixed. Melt margarine in a saucepan and add milk mixture. Bring to boil, stirring, and cook for 3 minutes; season to taste.
3 Add chicken to sauce and mix thoroughly; leave to cool.
4 Remove rind from bacon; lay rashers flat and divide chicken mixture between them. Roll up each rasher so that chicken is wrapped in bacon and forms a croquette; leave in a cool place.
5 Place all ingredients for batter in liquidiser goblet and run machine until well mixed.
6 Half fill deep-fat pan and put to heat.
7 Coat each croquette in batter and fry in deep fat for 6 to 8 minutes until golden brown; drain on kitchen paper. Pile on a warm serving dish, garnish with a sprig of parsley and serve piping hot.

5   CRISPY PORK CHOPS

For 4 portions:
3oz white bread
1 large orange
1 rounded tablespoon demerara sugar
1 rounded tablespoon thick honey
1 level teaspoon dry mustard
1 teaspoon Worcester sauce
4 pork chops
Fat for frying
1 (8oz) pack frozen peas

1 Remove crusts and break bread into small pieces;
place in liquidiser goblet a little at a time and run machine
until finely crumbed. Remove from liquidiser and place on
one side.
2 Cut 4 thin slices from orange and make a small cut into
the centre of each. Grate rind and squeeze juice from
remainder of orange.
3 Place rind and 1 tablespoon orange juice in liquidiser
goblet with demerara sugar, honey, mustard and Worcester
sauce and run machine until blended. Spread over pork
chops and coat them with breadcrumbs.
4 Heat a little fat in a frying pan and fry chops for 15 to 20
minutes, turning once, until golden brown on both sides;
drain on kitchen paper.
5 Cook peas, following directions on pack; drain and place
down the centre of a warm serving dish. Arrange chops on
peas and garnish each chop with a twist of orange.

2 5   PARSLEY AND LEMON STUFFING

4oz white bread, with crusts removed
1 small onion
Half a lemon
Large sprig of parsley
1 standard egg
$\frac{1}{2}$ level teaspoon salt
Pepper

1 Break bread into small pieces; place in liquidiser goblet
a little at a time and run machine until bread is crumbed;
turn into a bowl.
2 Peel and quarter onion. Place in liquidiser goblet and run
machine until onion is roughly chopped; add to bowl.
3 Grate rind of lemon and place in liquidiser goblet.
Squeeze juice and add to liquidiser goblet, together with
remaining ingredients; run machine until well blended. Pour
on to breadcrumbs and onion and stir to mix thoroughly.
4 Use to stuff a 3lb chicken (neck end) or form into balls
and bake for 20 to 25 minutes in a moderately hot oven
(400 deg F, Gas Mark 6).

2 5 6   BAKED MINCE LOAF

For 4 portions:
1 slice of bread, $\frac{1}{2}$in thick
1 medium-sized onion
$\frac{1}{4}$ level teaspoon mixed dried herbs
Salt and pepper
2 teaspoons of Worcester sauce
1 tablespoon tomato ketchup
1 standard egg
1lb minced beef

1 Prepare a moderate oven (350 deg F, Gas Mark 4).
2 Remove crusts and break bread into small pieces; place in
liquidiser goblet, a few at a time, and run machine until
bread is crumbed; turn into a 1-pint ovenproof basin.
3 Peel and cut onion into quarters, then place in liquidiser
goblet. Add remaining ingredients, except meat, and run
machine until onion is chopped. Add, with meat, to
breadcrumbs. Mix well, then press down firmly. Bake for
1 hour.
4 Drain off excess fat, turn out loaf on to a warm serving
dish and serve with gravy or tomato sauce.

1 2 3 5   CELERY AND HAM SOUFFLE

For 3 portions:
1 large (15oz) can celery hearts
$\frac{1}{4}$lb lean cooked ham
3 standard eggs
$\frac{1}{4}$ pint milk
1oz plain flour
1oz butter
$\frac{1}{2}$ level teaspoon salt
$\frac{1}{2}$ level teaspoon made mustard
Pepper

1 Prepare a moderate oven (375 deg F, Gas Mark 5).
Grease a 2-pint soufflé dish.
2 Thoroughly drain celery hearts and dry on kitchen paper;
place in soufflé dish. Cut ham into small dice.
3 Separate eggs and place yolks in liquidiser goblet and
whites in mixer bowl (clean and grease free). Add milk and
flour to liquidiser and run machine until blended.
4 Melt butter in a saucepan and add milk mixture. Bring to
boil, stirring continuously; cook for 2 minutes. Remove from
heat and add ham and seasonings.
5 Run mixer and whisk egg whites until stiff but not dry.
Beat a tablespoon of whites into the sauce and then fold in
remainder, using a metal spoon.
6 Pour into prepared dish and bake in the centre of oven for
35 to 40 minutes until well risen and golden brown. Serve
immediately.

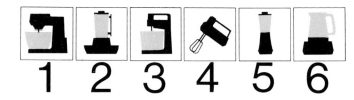

1 2 3 4 6

SPICY COBBLESTONE CASSEROLE

For 3 portions:
1 large onion
1 green pepper
2 level teaspoons tomato purée
2 level teaspoons paprika
1 level teaspoon sugar
$\frac{1}{2}$ level teaspoon salt
$\frac{1}{4}$ level teaspoon pepper
$\frac{1}{2}$ to $\frac{3}{4}$ pint stock or water
1lb stewing steak

COBBLER TOPPING
6oz self-raising flour
1 level teaspoon salt
2oz margarine
Milk to mix

2 rounded teaspoons cornflour

1 Peel onion, cut into quarters and place in liquidiser goblet.
2 Remove white pith and seeds from green pepper, cut into quarters and add to liquidiser.
3 Place tomato purée, paprika, sugar and seasonings in liquidiser with water; run machine until onion and pepper are finely chopped. Pour into a shallow 3-pint casserole.
4 Cut stewing steak into neat 1in pieces and add to casserole; cover and leave for 4 hours.
5 Place casserole in centre of oven. Turn oven setting to 325 deg F, Gas Mark 3, and cook for 2 hours, then increase heat to 400 deg F, Gas Mark 6.
6 Place flour and salt in mixer bowl. Add margarine, cut into small pieces, and run machine until mixture resembles fine breadcrumbs. Add milk and mix to a soft dough with a fork. Turn on to a floured board, roll out to $\frac{3}{4}$in thickness and cut into 1$\frac{1}{2}$in rounds.
7 Remove casserole from oven. Place cornflour in a small bowl and blend with a little water and stir into casserole.
8 Arrange cobbler rounds on top of casserole and return to oven, without lid. Cook for 20 minutes. Serve hot.

2 5 6

TOAD-IN-THE-HOLE

For 4 portions:
1oz lard or dripping
1lb pork sausages
4oz plain flour
1 level teaspoon salt
1 standard egg
$\frac{1}{2}$ pint milk and water mixed

1 Prepare a hot oven (425 deg F, Gas Mark 7). Put lard and sausages in a 7in by 11in roasting tin; place on top shelf of oven.
2 Place flour, salt, egg and milk and water in liquidiser goblet and run machine until thoroughly mixed; pour over sausages.
3 Bake in top of oven for 35 to 40 minutes until well risen, crisp and golden brown. Serve hot with vegetables.

2 6

PLAICE SOLANGE

For 4 portions:
MUSHROOM STUFFING
1 small onion
4oz mushrooms
$\frac{1}{2}$oz margarine
2oz white bread
Sprig of parsley
Salt and pepper

1 large (13oz) carton frozen small plaice fillets
Milk
1oz margarine
1oz plain flour
1 teaspoon lemon juice (optional)
1 (8oz) packet frozen mixed vegetables

1 Prepare a moderate oven (375 deg F, Gas Mark 5). Grease a shallow ovenproof dish.
2 Prepare stuffing: Peel and quarter onion, wash mushrooms, and place in liquidiser goblet; run machine until finely chopped. Melt margarine in a small saucepan; add onion and mushrooms and cook for 5 minutes. Remove crusts from bread and break into small pieces; place parsley in liquidiser goblet and run machine, adding bread a little at a time until crumbed. Stir into mushroom mixture with a little salt and pepper.
3 Separate fillets; when thawed, remove skins. Place fish skins in a pan with $\frac{1}{2}$ pint water and simmer for 10 minutes, then strain.
4 Place a little stuffing on each fillet and fold in half. Place in ovenproof dish and cover with lid, foil or greased greaseproof paper; bake in centre of oven for 15 to 20 minutes. When cooked, lift on to a serving dish and keep hot. Add any liquor to fish stock and make up to $\frac{1}{2}$ pint with milk.
5 Melt margarine in a small saucepan. Place flour and fish stock in liquidiser and run machine until blended; pour on to margarine and bring to boil, stirring, and cook for 2 minutes. Add lemon juice and season to taste with salt and pepper. Coat fish with sauce.
6 Cook mixed vegetables as directed on packet and arrange in centre of dish. Serve immediately.

Glazed Apricot-Stuffed Pork

This celebration roast pork joint is easier to prepare than it looks. Apricots give the stuffing and sauce a special tang that is delicious with pork

2 5   BAKED STUFFED HADDOCK

For 4 portions:
LEMON STUFFING
3oz white bread
Large sprig of parsley
Half a small lemon
2oz butter, melted
1 standard egg
½ level teaspoon mixed dried herbs
Pinch each of salt and pepper

---

1 large (13oz) carton frozen haddock steaks
Salt and pepper
2 medium-sized tomatoes
½oz margarine

1 Prepare a moderate oven (375 deg F, Gas Mark 5). Grease a shallow ovenproof dish.
2 Remove crusts and break bread into small pieces; place parsley in liquidiser goblet a little at a time and run machine, adding bread until finely crumbed.
3 Grate rind and squeeze juice from lemon; add to breadcrumbs with butter, egg, herbs and salt and pepper. Run machine until well mixed.
4 Place haddock steaks in ovenproof dish; season and cover with lemon stuffing. Slice tomatoes and arrange slices on top of stuffing. Dot tomato slices with margarine and bake in centre of oven for 30 to 40 minutes. Serve with peas and potatoes.

---

2 5 6   GLAZED APRICOT-STUFFED PORK
(pictured on pages 38, 39)

For 8 portions:
4lb loin of pork, chined

STUFFING
4oz white bread, with crusts removed
Large sprig of parsley
1 large (15oz) can apricot halves
½ level teaspoon mixed dried herbs
1 standard egg
Salt and pepper

---

2 level tablespoons demerara sugar

SAUCE
¾lb cooking apples
6 tablespoons water
1 rounded tablespoon granulated sugar, or to taste

---

8 tomatoes
1 (8oz) packet frozen peas
1 cauliflower
Duchesse Potatoes (see recipe right)

1 Carefully remove skin from pork, leaving fat intact. Remove bones and cut through fat down centre of loin; ease fat away, for about 1in, from meat on each side of centre cut.
2 Score fat in a diamond pattern with a sharp knife.
3 Break bread into small pieces, place in liquidiser goblet, with parsley, and run machine until bread is finely crumbed and parsley is chopped; place in a bowl. Drain apricots, place half in liquidiser goblet and run machine until roughly chopped; add to bowl with herbs, egg and seasonings, and mix well to bind.
4 Prepare a moderate oven (375 deg F, Gas Mark 5).
5 Press stuffing in cut in fat on top of loin; place loin in a roasting tin and pour the apricot syrup over. Sprinkle fat with demerara sugar, pressing well into score marks and cook for 1½ hours, basting occasionally with apricot syrup. Cover stuffing with a strip of foil to prevent surface from becoming overbrowned, then cook for a further 1 hour.
6 Peel, quarter and core apples and place in a saucepan with water and sugar; cook until tender. Place in liquidiser goblet with remaining apricots and run machine until smooth and well blended. Return to saucepan and re-heat just before serving.
7 Cut a slice from rounded end of each tomato; scoop out seeds. Place tomato shells in a small ovenproof dish and cook in oven for 5 minutes.
8 Cook peas as directed on packet; drain and pile into tomato shells.
9 Wash cauliflower, break into small sprigs and cook in boiling, salted water until tender; drain thoroughly.
10 Place pork on a serving dish; arrange some tomatoes, cauliflower sprigs and Duchesse Potatoes around. Serve remaining vegetables separately. Serve with apple and apricot sauce.

---

1 3 4   DUCHESSE POTATOES

For 8 portions:
3lb potatoes
Milk
2oz butter
2 standard eggs
Salt and pepper
A little melted butter to glaze

1 Peel potatoes, cook in boiling, salted water until tender; drain and dry over a low heat.
2 Place in mixer bowl and run machine until potatoes are broken down; add milk, 2oz butter, eggs and seasonings; beat thoroughly.
3 Place in a piping bag fitted with a large star tube, and pipe whirls on to a greased baking sheet. Brush with melted butter and place in oven with joint for 20 to 30 minutes, until lightly browned.

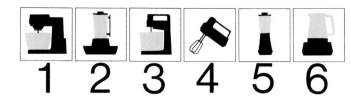

1 2 3 4 5 6

2   STUFFED BREASTS OF LAMB

For 4 portions:
2 breasts of lamb

STUFFING
4 large slices white bread
2oz mushroom stalks
1 medium-sized cooking apple
Salt and pepper
2 tablespoons milk

1oz cooking fat
2 medium-sized onions
½ pint water
1 beef extract cube
1 level tablespoon cornflour

1 Ask the butcher to bone breasts of lamb. Remove crusts from bread. Place bread and mushroom stalks in liquidiser goblet a little at a time and run machine until bread is crumbed; turn out into a small bowl. Peel, quarter and core apple. Place in liquidiser goblet and run machine until roughly chopped. Add bread mixture, a little seasoning and milk to liquidiser and run machine until just blended.
2 Place half the stuffing on each piece of meat; roll up and tie securely with string.
3 Melt fat in a large saucepan and brown meat quickly all over. Lift out on to a plate.
4 Peel and slice onions; add to pan and fry for about 5 minutes. Add water and beef extract cube. Bring to boil and return meat to pan; cover and simmer for 1½ hours.
5 Lift meat on to a serving dish; remove string and keep meat hot in a low oven. Skim fat from surface of gravy. Blend cornflour with a little water and add to pan; cook for 3 minutes. Pour gravy over meat and serve.

1 2 3 5 6

SMOKED HADDOCK FLAN

For 4 portions:
¾lb smoked haddock fillet
1lb potatoes
1 standard egg
2oz butter
½ pint milk
1oz plain flour
Salt and pepper
2 tomatoes
1 tablespoon mayonnaise

1 Wash fish and place in a shallow pan. Cover with water and simmer for 8 to 10 minutes until tender. Drain and remove skin; flake fish.
2 Wash and peel potatoes. Cook in boiling, salted water until tender, then drain and dry over low heat; place in mixer bowl. Run machine until potatoes are broken down.
3 Separate egg; add yolk to potatoes and place whites in a clean, grease-free bowl. Prepare a medium grill.
4 Add 1oz butter to potatoes and run machine, to mix well. Spread potatoes over base and sides of an 8in pie plate. Place under grill for 8 minutes.
5 Place milk and flour in liquidiser goblet and run machine until blended. Melt remaining butter in a saucepan and add milk mixture. Bring to boil, stirring, and cook for 3 minutes. Stir in flaked fish. Season to taste.
6 Slice tomatoes and place over base of potato case. Cover with smoked haddock mixture.
7 Whisk egg white until stiff but not dry; fold in mayonnaise and spread over smoked haddock. Place under grill until golden brown, then serve.

2 5   STUFFED BEEF ROLLS

For 4 portions:
4 slices braising steak (about 1lb in weight)
4 small onions

STUFFING
3oz white bread
Half a small lemon
Salt and pepper
1 level teaspoon dried sage
1 standard egg

1oz lard or dripping
1 beef extract cube
½ pint water
1 level tablespoon cornflour

1 Place each slice of meat between 2 small pieces of greaseproof paper and beat with a rolling pin until thin. Peel and slice onions.
2 Remove crusts and break bread into pieces; place in liquidiser goblet a little at a time and run machine until bread is crumbed. Grate rind and squeeze juice from lemon; add to breadcrumbs with seasonings, sage and egg; run machine until well mixed.
3 Divide stuffing into 4. Place a portion of stuffing on each piece of meat and roll up tightly; tie securely with cotton.
4 Melt lard in a saucepan or frying pan with a lid. Brown meat quickly all over and remove from pan. Add sliced onions and fry for 3 minutes; add beef extract cube and water to pan. Replace meat and cover pan; simmer for 1½ hours.
5 Arrange beef rolls on a warm serving dish; remove cotton and keep rolls warm.
7 Blend cornflour with a little water. Stir into gravy in pan and cook for 3 minutes, stirring. Pour over beef rolls and serve.

Salmon, Cheese and Tomato Flan
Make this flan for an economical family meal. You can serve it hot or cold, with salad

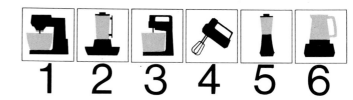

1 3 SMOKED HADDOCK FISH CAKES

For 3 portions:
$\frac{3}{4}$lb potatoes
$\frac{1}{2}$lb smoked haddock fillet
1 level tablespoon chopped parsley
Salt and pepper
Beaten egg
Browned breadcrumbs
Fat for frying

1 Wash and peel potatoes. Cook in boiling, salted water until tender, then drain and dry over low heat; place in mixer bowl. Run machine until lightly mashed.
2 Wash fish and place in a shallow pan. Cover with water and simmer for 8 to 10 minutes until tender; drain and remove skin. Add fish to potato, with parsley, and run machine until mixed. Season to taste.
3 Shape mixture into 6 flat cakes and coat each in beaten egg and breadcrumbs.
4 Heat a little fat in a frying pan and fry cakes for 2 to 3 minutes on each side until golden brown; drain on kitchen paper.
5 Serve with Fresh Tomato Sauce (see page 88) and peas.

1 2 3 4 5

SALMON, CHEESE AND TOMATO FLAN
(pictured left and on back cover)

For 4 or 5 portions:
SHORTCRUST PASTRY
4oz plain flour
$\frac{1}{4}$ level teaspoon salt
1oz cooking fat
1oz margarine
Cold water to mix

FILLING
$\frac{1}{2}$oz plain flour
$\frac{1}{4}$ pint milk
3oz Cheddar cheese
$\frac{1}{2}$oz margarine
Salt and pepper
1 small (7$\frac{1}{2}$oz) can pink salmon
2 tomatoes

1 Prepare a hot oven (425 deg F, Gas Mark 7).
2 Make pastry as directed on page 7.
3 Roll out pastry on a floured board and line a 7in plain flan ring or sponge tin. Prick base with a fork.
4 Place a circle of greaseproof paper in flan and fill with baking beans or rice. Bake in centre of oven for 15 minutes. Remove beans and paper and cook for a further 5 minutes.

5 To make filling: Place flour and milk in liquidiser goblet. Cut 2oz of cheese into $\frac{3}{4}$in dice and add to liquidiser goblet. Run machine until cheese is broken down.
6 Melt margarine in a small saucepan, add contents of liquidiser goblet and stir over moderate heat until sauce thickens and boils. Simmer, stirring, for 2 minutes. Add seasonings, and stir in liquor from salmon can.
7 Flake salmon, discard bones and stir fish into sauce; pour into flan case. Grate remaining 1oz cheese; sprinkle over filling. Slice tomatoes, cut each slice in half and arrange around edge of flan. Brown cheese under a medium grill. Serve hot, or cold, with salad.

2 BRAISED STUFFED VEAL

For 4 to 6 portions:
1$\frac{1}{2}$lb to 2lb breast of veal

STUFFING
1 small onion
1oz margarine
4oz white bread
Large sprig of parsley
$\frac{1}{4}$lb mushrooms
Salt and pepper
1 standard egg, beaten

3 or 4 sticks of celery
Water

1 Ask butcher to bone breast of veal. Prepare a moderate oven (350 deg F, Gas Mark 4).
2 Peel and quarter onion; place in liquidiser goblet and run machine until roughly chopped. Melt margarine in a small saucepan; add onion, cover, and cook without browning for 8 to 10 minutes, until soft.
3 Remove crusts and break bread into small pieces; place parsley in liquidiser goblet and run machine, adding bread a little at a time, until finely crumbed. Remove and place in a small basin.
4 Wash and dry mushrooms; break into quarters, add to liquidiser goblet and run machine until roughly chopped. Add to pan and cook for 3 minutes. Stir in breadcrumbs and parsley, seasonings and beaten egg; mix well.
5 Lay veal flat and spread stuffing over; roll up and secure with string. Place veal in a casserole.
6 Wash celery and slice; place around veal. Add sufficient water to cover base of casserole and sprinkle veal with salt and pepper. Cover casserole, place in oven and cook for 1$\frac{1}{2}$ hours.
7 To serve: Place meat on a serving dish; spoon celery around meat and serve gravy in a gravy boat.

2 6 BEEFBURGERS WITH TOMATO SAUCE

For 3 portions:
1 large onion
2 or 3 sticks celery
3oz white bread
¾lb minced beef
Salt and pepper
1 teaspoon Worcester sauce
1 standard egg
Plain flour
Fat for frying
1 large (14oz) can peeled tomatoes
2 to 3 tablespoons water
1 (8oz) pack frozen green beans

1 Peel and quarter onion. Wash celery and cut into short
lengths. Place celery and onion in liquidiser goblet and run
machine until roughly chopped; place in a bowl.
2 Remove crusts and break bread into small pieces; place
in liquidiser goblet a little at a time and run machine until
finely crumbed. Add to bowl with minced beef, seasonings,
Worcester sauce and egg. Beat together until
thoroughly mixed.
3 Turn mixture on to a floured board and shape into 6
cakes; coat in flour.
4 Melt a little fat in a large frying pan and fry beefburgers
for 6 to 8 minutes on each side.
5 Drain excess fat from pan and add contents of can of
tomatoes and water. Bring to boil, season, and cook for 2
to 3 minutes.
6 Cook beans as directed on pack; drain.
7 Arrange beefburgers on a warm serving dish; spoon over
the tomato sauce and serve with sliced green beans.

2 DEVILLED KIDNEYS

For 4 portions:
8 lambs' kidneys
1 onion
3 rashers back bacon
½oz margarine
¼lb mushrooms
1 large (15oz) can tomatoes
1 tablespoon Worcester sauce
1 tablespoon vinegar
1 level teaspoon dry mustard
Salt and pepper
1 rounded tablespoon plain flour
Chopped parsley

1 Remove fat and skin from kidneys; cut in halves and
remove cores.
2 Peel and quarter onion; place in liquidiser goblet and run
machine until roughly chopped. Remove rind from bacon
and cut into strips.
3 Melt margarine in a frying pan and fry bacon and onion
for 2 to 3 minutes; add kidneys and fry for 2 minutes.
4 Wash mushrooms and break into rough pieces;
add to pan.
5 Place remaining ingredients, except parsley, in liquidiser
goblet and run machine until well blended. Add to pan
and bring to boil, stirring; reduce heat and simmer
for 15 minutes.
6 Turn into a warm serving dish, sprinkle with chopped
parsley and serve with boiled rice.

1 2 5 6 UPSIDE-DOWN LAYERED PIE

For 4 portions:
1½lb potatoes
Milk
Salt and pepper
4oz white bread
1½oz margarine
1 onion
1 carrot
1oz dripping
1lb minced beef
1 rounded tablespoon plain flour
1 small (8oz) can baked beans with tomato sauce
1 tomato
Sprig of parsley

1 Prepare a moderate oven (350 deg F, Gas Mark 4).
Grease an oblong 3-pint casserole.
2 Wash and peel potatoes and cook in boiling, salted water
until tender; drain and dry over low heat. Place in mixer
bowl, run machine and mash with a little milk and seasonings.
3 Remove crusts and break bread into small pieces; place
in liquidiser goblet a little at a time and run machine until
crumbed.
4 Heat margarine in a frying pan and fry breadcrumbs until
golden brown; place in base of casserole.
5 Peel and quarter onion. Wash carrot and cut into small
pieces. Place onion and carrot in liquidiser goblet and run
machine until roughly chopped. (If using a small liquidiser,
chop the vegetables by hand.)
6 Melt dripping in frying pan and fry onion, carrot and
minced beef for 10 minutes, stirring continuously. Stir in
flour, baked beans and some seasonings.
7 Place half of the mashed potato in casserole on top of
breadcrumbs; cover with minced beef and, finally, remaining
potato. Press down well. Bake in centre of oven for 35
minutes. Turn out on to a flat ovenproof serving dish.
8 Slice tomato, arrange on top and return to oven for
5 minutes. Garnish with sprig of parsley and serve.

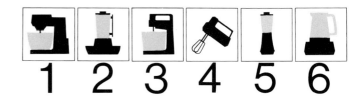

2 5 6 CHEESE-STUFFED PANCAKES

For 3 portions:
BATTER
4oz plain flour
½ level teaspoon salt
1 standard egg
½ pint milk
Lard or cooking oil for frying

FILLING
5oz Cheddar cheese
1oz plain flour
½ pint milk
Salt and pepper
1oz margarine
1 (7oz) can peeled prawns

1 Make up pancake batter, following directions on page 17.
2 Make 6 large pancakes, using lard or cooking oil for frying. Stack on a plate and keep warm.
3 Cut 4oz cheese into ¾in cubes. Place cheese, flour and milk in liquidiser goblet; season with salt and pepper. Run machine until cheese is broken down.
4 Melt margarine in a saucepan, add contents of liquidiser goblet and stir over moderate heat until sauce comes to boil; simmer, stirring, for 2 minutes.
5 Prepare a hot grill. Drain liquid from prawns, rinse prawns with cold water, drain and stir into sauce. Fill pancakes and roll up. Place in a shallow ovenproof dish and pour any remaining sauce over pancakes. Grate remaining cheese on top. Place under grill until brown and bubbling.
Serve piping hot.

1 2 6 MEAT BALLS FARMHOUSE STYLE

For 4 portions:
2oz white bread
1lb minced beef
1 standard egg
Salt and pepper
Pinch of mixed dried herbs
Plain flour
1oz margarine

SAUCE
1 large onion
1 large carrot
1 beef extract cube
½ pint water
1 rounded tablespoon tomato purée
Salt and pepper
1 rounded tablespoon cornflour
1 small (5oz) can garden peas

1 Remove crusts and break bread into small pieces; place in liquidiser goblet a little at a time and run machine until finely crumbed. Place in mixer bowl with minced beef, egg, a little salt and pepper and herbs; run machine until well mixed. Turn on to a floured board, shape into 16 balls and coat in flour.
2 Melt margarine in a frying pan and fry meat balls until golden brown all over; lift out on to a plate.
3 Peel and quarter onion. Peel carrot and cut in pieces. Place onion and carrot in liquidiser goblet and run machine until roughly chopped. Add to fat remaining in pan and fry slowly for 5 minutes. Add beef extract cube, water and tomato purée; bring to boil and season to taste. Return meat balls to pan, cover with a lid or foil and simmer for 25 minutes.
4 Blend cornflour with a little cold water and stir into sauce. Drain peas, add to pan and heat for 2 to 3 minutes. Adjust seasoning and serve with creamed potatoes.

1 3 4 SALMON AND CORN FLAN

For 4 portions:
PASTRY
6oz plain flour
Salt
1½oz margarine
1½oz lard
Cold water to mix

FILLING
1 small (7oz) can red salmon
1 small (7oz) can sweet corn niblets
Milk
2 standard eggs, beaten
Salt and pepper

1 Prepare a moderately hot oven (400 deg F, Gas Mark 6).
2 Sift flour and salt into mixer bowl; add fats, cut in small pieces, and run mixer until mixture resembles fine breadcrumbs. Mix in sufficient water with a fork to make a stiff dough.
3 Roll out pastry and line an 8in, deep pie plate; trim and flute edges.
4 Drain liquids from cans of salmon and sweet corn and make up to ¼ pint with milk; place in mixer bowl.
5 Remove skin and bones from salmon. Add salmon, sweet corn and eggs to mixer bowl and mix together. Season to taste.
6 Pour into pastry case and bake in centre of oven for 25 to 30 minutes until set and a light golden brown. Serve either hot or cold.

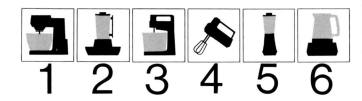

2 5 6   SURPRISE PIES

Makes 4 pies:
FILLING
¼ pint chicken stock
¾oz plain flour
¾oz margarine
6oz diced cooked chicken
2 to 3 tablespoons cooked mixed vegetables, sweet
    corn or peas
Salt and pepper

PASTRY
8oz plain flour
Salt
2oz margarine
2oz lard
Cold water to mix

2 hard-boiled eggs
Milk

1 Prepare a moderately hot oven (400 deg F, Gas Mark 6).
2 Place stock and flour in liquidiser goblet and run machine until well blended. Melt margarine in a saucepan and add stock mixture; bring to boil, stirring, and cook for 3 minutes. Add chicken, vegetables and seasonings; mix well.
3 Sift flour and salt into mixer bowl; add fats, cut into small pieces, and run mixer until mixture resembles fine bread-crumbs. Add sufficient water to make a stiff dough.
4 Roll out pastry and line 4 (3½in) individual pie tins; roll out 4 circles for lids.
5 Cut eggs in halves and place 1 half in each pastry case. Divide filling between cases. Dampen edges of pastry lids and cover pies. Make a slit in the top of each pie; brush with milk and bake in centre of oven for 30 minutes.
Serve either hot or cold.

2 6   CROWNED COD STEAKS
(pictured right)

For 4 portions:
Butter
4 cod steaks

STUFFING
2oz white bread, with crusts removed
Large sprig of parsley
2 hard-boiled eggs
1oz margarine
1 small (2oz) carton peeled prawns
Salt and pepper

Parsley to garnish
Hollandaise Sauce (see page 83 for recipe)

1 Prepare a moderate oven (375 deg F, Gas Mark 5).
2 Thickly butter a shallow ovenproof dish. Wash and trim cod steaks, dry on kitchen paper and place in dish.
3 Break bread into small pieces and place in liquidiser goblet with parsley; run machine until bread is finely crumbed and parsley chopped; place on a plate. Add eggs to liquidiser and run machine until roughly chopped.
4 Melt margarine in a small saucepan and add breadcrumbs and parsley, eggs, prawns and seasonings to taste; mix well, then pile on to cod steaks.
5 Bake in centre of oven for 25 minutes. Garnish dish with parsley. Serve hot with Hollandaise Sauce.

1 3 4   FARMHOUSE BEEF ROLL

For 3 portions:
1 small onion
8oz minced beef
1 (10oz) can condensed tomato soup
½ level teaspoon mixed dried herbs (optional)
½ level teaspoon salt
¼ level teaspoon pepper

SCONE DOUGH
8oz self-raising flour
1 level teaspoon salt
2oz margarine
Milk

3 tablespoons water
Worcester sauce

1 Prepare a hot oven (425 deg F, Gas Mark 7). Lightly grease a baking sheet.
2 Peel and chop onion. Place onion and minced beef in a saucepan and fry slowly until meat is browned.
3 Add 3 level tablespoons of soup from can, mixed herbs (if used), salt and pepper; mix well.
4 Place flour and salt in mixer bowl. Add margarine, cut into pieces, and run machine until mixture resembles fine breadcrumbs. Add about 7 to 8 tablespoons of milk and mix to a soft dough.
5 Turn out on to a floured board and roll out to an oblong, 12in by 10in. Place meat filling down centre of dough; dampen edges and fold dough over filling in centre. Invert roll and place, folded side downwards, on baking sheet.
6 Brush with milk and bake in centre of oven for 30 minutes until golden brown; place on a warm serving dish and keep hot.
7 Place 3 tablespoons of water, a few drops of Worcester sauce and remaining soup in a small saucepan. Bring to boil, stirring, and cook for 2 minutes. Serve hot with beef roll.

Crowned Cod Steaks

The delicious stuffing for these cod steaks is quickly made in the liquidiser. Serve with Hollandaise Sauce, also made in the liquidiser, and buttered carrots

2 5 SPIT-ROASTED CHICKEN WITH BARBECUE SAUCE

For 4 portions:
1 (3lb) roasting chicken
1 small onion
3 level tablespoons tomato purée
Dash of Worcester sauce
1 tablespoon vinegar
1 level teaspoon dry mustard
1 level teaspoon mixed spice

1 Remove giblets from chicken and simmer in a little water to make stock. Prepare a hot grill.
2 Peel and quarter onion; place in liquidiser goblet, add remaining ingredients, plus 6 tablespoonsful of giblet stock, and run machine until onion is chopped.
3 Place chicken firmly on spit and baste well with the sauce. Cook for 10 minutes at full heat; lower heat and cook for a further 50 minutes, basting occasionally.
4 Remove chicken from spit and place on a warm serving dish.
5 Make up remaining stock to $\frac{1}{4}$ pint and add to any sauce remaining in drip pan and stir well to mix. Bring to boil and pour over chicken or serve in a sauce boat.

1 2 3 4 5 TUNA HORSESHOE

For 4 portions:
1 (7oz) can tuna steak
Milk
$\frac{3}{4}$oz margarine
$\frac{3}{4}$oz plain flour
1 small (5oz) can garden peas
Salt and pepper

SCONE MIXTURE
6oz self-raising flour
$\frac{1}{2}$ level teaspoon salt
2oz margarine
Cold water to mix

Beaten egg to glaze
4 tomatoes

1 Prepare a moderately hot oven (400 deg F, Gas Mark 6).
2 Drain liquor from tuna and make up to $\frac{1}{4}$ pint with milk; flake fish.
3 Melt margarine in a small saucepan. Place flour and milk in liquidiser goblet and run machine until well mixed. Pour into pan and bring to boil, stirring; cook for 3 minutes.
4 Drain garden peas and add to sauce, with fish; season to taste.

5 Place self-raising flour and salt in mixer bowl, add margarine, cut into small pieces, and run machine until mixture resembles fine breadcrumbs; mix in sufficient water with a fork to make a firm dough. Turn on to a floured board.
6 Roll out to an oblong, 9in by 12in. Spread tuna filling over dough to within $\frac{3}{4}$in of edges. Dampen long edges and roll up, Swiss-roll fashion. Place on a baking sheet and form into a horseshoe. Make 4 diagonal cuts along the top.
7 Brush with beaten egg and bake in the centre of oven for 15 minutes. Halve tomatoes, place on baking sheet and cook for a further 10 minutes.
8 Place horseshoe on a serving dish and fill the centre with tomato halves.

2 5 6 ITALIAN HAM BAKE

For 4 portions:
4oz long-grain rice
4oz mushrooms
1oz margarine
1 large (14oz) can peeled tomatoes
1 level teaspoon sugar
Celery salt
Salt and pepper

CHEESE SAUCE
5oz Cheddar cheese
1oz plain flour
$\frac{1}{2}$ pint milk
1 level teaspoon salt
Pepper
$\frac{1}{2}$ level teaspoon dry mustard
1oz margarine

8oz sliced cooked ham

1 Prepare a moderate oven (350 deg F, Gas Mark 4).
2 Cook rice in boiling, salted water for about 12 minutes until tender. Drain in a sieve or colander and rinse in cold water.
3 Wash and slice mushrooms. Melt margarine in a saucepan, add mushrooms and cook for 5 minutes. Add rice, drained tomatoes and sugar. Season with celery salt, salt and pepper; stir and remove from heat.
4 Make cheese sauce: Cut 4oz of the cheese into $\frac{3}{4}$in dice and place in liquidiser goblet with the flour, milk, salt, pepper and mustard; run machine until cheese is broken down. Melt margarine in a saucepan. Add cheese mixture and cook over a moderate heat until sauce boils. Simmer, stirring, for 2 minutes.
5 Place a third of the ham in the base of a 2-pint deep, square, or oblong, ovenproof dish. Spread over half the rice

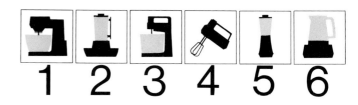

mixture and cover with another third of the ham. Top with remaining rice mixture. Arrange remaining ham on top and pour cheese sauce over. Grate remaining cheese and sprinkle over sauce.

6 Place on a baking sheet and bake in centre of oven for 40 minutes, until golden brown. Serve piping hot.

---

1 2 3 4 5 6
GOOD FRIDAY FISH PIE

For 4 portions:
1½lb potatoes
Milk
Butter
Salt and pepper
2 standard eggs
¾lb cod fillet
½ pint milk
1oz plain flour
4 or 5 sprigs of parsley
1 (7oz) can tuna steak

1 Prepare a moderate oven (375 deg F, Gas Mark 5).
2 Peel potatoes, cook in boiling, salted water until tender; drain and dry over low heat.
3 Place in mixer bowl and run machine until potatoes are broken down; add milk, 1oz butter and seasonings and beat until creamy.
4 Hard boil eggs for 10 minutes; crack and leave in cold water to cool. Shell and dry on kitchen paper; chop roughly.
5 Place cod on a board, skin side downwards, and cut fish off skin with a large knife. Cut fish into cubes.
6 Place milk and flour in liquidiser goblet and run machine until well blended. Melt 1oz butter in a medium-sized saucepan, add contents of liquidiser goblet and stir over moderate heat until sauce boils. Simmer, stirring for 2 minutes. Return sauce to liquidiser, add parsley sprigs and run machine until parsley is chopped.
7 Return sauce to saucepan, add seasonings to taste, then stir in contents of can of tuna. Beat to break down tuna. Mix in cubed cod and hard-boiled egg and pour into a 2-pint or 2½-pint ovenproof dish. Cover with creamed potato and mark the surface with a fork. Dot with butter, then place dish on a baking sheet and bake at the top of oven for about 40 minutes until potato is golden brown. Serve with peas.

NOTE: When using a large liquidiser, place parsley in liquidiser goblet with milk and flour and run machine until parsley is chopped. It is then unnecessary to return sauce to liquidiser with parsley.

---

2 5 6   TASTY STUFFED PLAICE

For 4 portions:
1½lb small plaice fillets

STUFFING
2oz white bread, with crusts removed
2 sprigs of parsley
½ level teaspoon dried marjoram
Grated rind of half a lemon
Salt and pepper
5 tablespoons milk

SAUCE
Fish liquor
Milk
½oz plain flour
½oz margarine
2 level tablespoons mayonnaise
Salt and pepper

1 Remove dark skin from plaice fillets and place skin (or skinned) sides uppermost on a board.
2 Break bread into pieces and place in liquidiser goblet, a little at a time, with parsley. Run machine until bread is crumbed, and parsley chopped. Turn into a bowl. Add marjoram, lemon rind and seasonings to breadcrumbs. Add milk and mix well together.
3 Spread stuffing on plaice fillets and roll up. Arrange on a buttered pie plate or soup plate; place over a saucepan of boiling water and cover with a plate or foil. Steam for 10 to 20 minutes, depending on size.
4 Remove from heat and arrange plaice on a warm serving dish, keep hot. Strain fish liquor from plaice into a measuring jug and make up to ½ pint with milk. Place in liquidiser goblet.
5 Add flour and run machine until well blended. Melt margarine in a saucepan. Add contents of liquidiser goblet, stir over a moderate heat until sauce comes to boil. Simmer, stirring, for 2 minutes. Stir in mayonnaise and season to taste.
6 Pour sauce over plaice and serve hot with fresh spinach or peas and creamed potatoes.

Hot and Cold Puddings

Gooseberry Ginger Cloud
Your liquidiser will make the fruit purée creamy smooth for this refreshing sweet. When gooseberries are not in season, use plums or apricots instead

Let your mixer and liquidiser do the work and produce fabulously light, fluffy, cold desserts and rich, extra-light puddings.

2 6   GOOSEBERRY GINGER CLOUD
(pictured left)

For 4 portions:
PUREE
1lb gooseberries
4 tablespoons water
4oz sugar

CUSTARD
3 standard eggs
1oz castor sugar
Pinch of salt
½ pint milk

4oz ginger biscuits
Green food colouring

1 Remove any leaves from gooseberries and top and tail fruit. Wash, then place in a saucepan with water and sugar. Bring to boil, cover and simmer for 15 to 20 minutes until fruit is well broken down. Place fruit in liquidiser goblet and run machine until fruit is smooth. Leave to cool. (Purée may be strained to remove seeds.)
2 Separate two of the eggs. Place whites in clean, grease-free mixer bowl and yolks in liquidiser goblet. Add whole egg to liquidiser with sugar, salt and milk. Run machine until well mixed. Pour into a saucepan and cook over a very low heat, stirring, until mixture thickens and coats back of spoon. Do not allow to boil. Remove from heat, pour into a basin and cover surface with wet greaseproof paper to prevent a skin forming. Leave to cool completely.
3 Break up ginger biscuits. Place, a little at a time, in grinder or liquidiser goblet and run machine until coarsely crushed.
4 Stir half of gooseberry purée into cooled custard. Tint with green food colouring. Divide between 4 individual glasses. Spoon a layer of crushed biscuits on top.
5 Whisk egg whites in mixer bowl until stiff, but not dry. Fold in remaining purée. Pile on top of biscuits in each glass.

2 5 6   RHUBARB FOOL

For 4 portions:
1lb rhubarb
3 rounded tablespoons sugar
3 tablespoons water
½ pint milk
1 rounded tablespoon custard powder
Pink food colouring
1 small (2⅞ fluid oz) carton double cream

1 Remove leaves and stalk ends from rhubarb and wipe with a cloth. Cut into 1in lengths and place in a saucepan with 2 rounded tablespoons of sugar and the water; cover

and stew until soft. Place rhubarb in liquidiser goblet and run machine until smooth.
2 Make custard with milk, custard powder and remaining sugar. When cooked, gradually beat in rhubarb purée. (If using a large liquidiser, add custard to rhubarb and run until well blended.)
3 Add a few drops of pink colouring, if necessary. Cool slightly, then place in a serving dish. Leave to cool; chill, if possible.
4 Whisk cream until stiff and pipe or fork around the edge of dish. Serve with shortbread finger biscuits.

2 6   CREAMY COFFEE MOULD

For 6 to 8 portions:
2 standard eggs
1oz cornflour
3oz castor sugar
1 level tablespoon instant coffee powder
1 level tablespoon drinking chocolate
¾ pint milk
3 tablespoons water
½oz (or 1 envelope) gelatine
1 small can evaporated milk

CHOCOLATE SAUCE
4 level tablespoons drinking chocolate
¼ pint water
½oz butter
2 tablespoons milk

1 Separate eggs. Place yolks in liquidiser goblet and whites in a clean, grease-free bowl. Add cornflour, sugar, coffee, drinking chocolate and a little milk to liquidiser goblet and run machine until well mixed. Put remaining milk on to heat.
2 Pour the hot milk on to coffee mixture and run machine until thoroughly blended. Return to pan, bring to boil, stirring continuously, and cook for 3 minutes. Remove from heat and leave to cool slightly. Measure 3 tablespoons cold water into a small basin and add gelatine. Place basin in a pan of water over moderate heat and stir until dissolved. Add, with evaporated milk, to coffee mixture, stirring in well.
4 Whisk egg whites until stiff, but not dry, and fold into coffee mixture. Turn into a 2-pint jelly mould; leave to set.
5 To make chocolate sauce: Place drinking chocolate and water in a saucepan. Bring to boil, stirring, then simmer, uncovered, over a low heat for 10 minutes, stirring occasionally. Remove from heat and stir in butter and milk. Allow to cool.
6 Dip mould into a bowl of hand-hot water and invert on to a serving dish. Pour over a little sauce, and serve remainder separately.

2 6   APRICOT FOAM

For 4 to 6 portions:
3 tablespoons cold water
½oz (or 1 envelope) gelatine
1 large (15oz) can apricot halves
2oz castor sugar
2 standard eggs
1 teaspoon lemon juice
1 small (6oz) can Danish cream

1 Measure water into a small basin and add gelatine.
2 Reserve 5 apricot halves for decoration. Place remainder in a saucepan with syrup from can and sugar. Bring to boil, then pour into liquidiser goblet. Add gelatine and run machine until mixture is smooth.
3 Separate eggs. Place whites in a clean, grease-free bowl, and yolks in liquidiser with apricot mixture, lemon juice and the cream; run machine until well mixed. Leave to cool in liquidiser in a cold place until almost set, then run machine until foamy.
4 Whisk egg whites until stiff, but not dry. Fold in fruit mixture and pour into a 2-pint mould and leave to set in a cold place.
5 Just before serving, dip mould into hand-hot water and invert on to a serving dish. Decorate with apricot halves.

2 5   ORANGE CHEESECAKE

For 6 to 8 portions:
3 tablespoons cold water
½oz (or 1 envelope) gelatine
2oz butter
6oz digestive biscuits
2oz demerara sugar
¼ pint boiling water
1 large orange
1 lemon
1lb cottage cheese
6 level tablespoons castor sugar

DECORATION
2 oranges
1 small (2⅞ fluid oz) carton double cream
Angelica

1 Grease a 6½in deep cake tin with a loose base. Measure 3 tablespoonsful of cold water into a small basin and add gelatine.
2 Melt butter in a small saucepan. Place biscuits, a few at a time, in grinder or liquidiser goblet and run machine until reduced to fine crumbs. Place in a bowl and add demerara sugar and butter. Mix well. Press biscuit mixture into

base of tin and leave in a cool place to harden. Place gelatine and boiling water in liquidiser and run machine until gelatine has melted.
3 Cut 3 thin strips of rind from orange and lemon and add to liquidiser. Remove the skin and pith from orange and lemon, cut fruit into pieces, place in liquidiser and run until well blended. Strain into a jug.
4 Place cottage cheese, castor sugar and fruit juice in liquidiser and run until well blended. Pour on to biscuit base and leave in a cool place until set. (If using a small liquidiser, blend half the cottage cheese, half the fruit juice and half the sugar at a time.)
5 When set, push up base of tin, carefully remove tin base and place cheesecake, crumb.side downwards, on a serving dish.
6 To decorate: Remove peel and pith from oranges with a small, sharp or serrated knife, and cut out orange segments from between pith. Drain on kitchen paper. Place some segments radiating from centre of cake and remainder around edge of serving dish. Whisk cream until thick, and pipe or fork in stars around edge of cheesecake. Place a small piece of angelica on top of each star.

2 5 6   COTTAGE PLUM CRUNCH

For 4 portions:
1oz soft brown sugar
1oz butter
4 rounded tablespoons cornflakes
1lb ripe plums
4 tablespoons water
3 level tablespoons castor sugar
4oz stale sponge cake
1 (2oz) carton dessert topping mix
4 fluid oz milk

1 Place brown sugar and butter in a small saucepan and heat together until sugar has melted. Stir in cornflakes and leave to cool.
2 Cut plums in halves, remove stones, and place in a saucepan with water and sugar. Bring to boil, cover, and simmer for 5 to 10 minutes until plums have broken down.
3 Place in liquidiser goblet and run machine until smooth. (It may be necessary to divide into 2 batches.)
4 Cut sponge cake into small dice. Divide evenly between individual glasses or fruit dishes. Divide plum purée between glasses and leave to cool.
5 Make up dessert topping mix with milk, following directions on carton. Pile a layer of topping on each portion. Spoon crunchy cornflake mixture on top and serve at once.
NOTE: Use apples, apricots or gooseberries when plums are not in season.

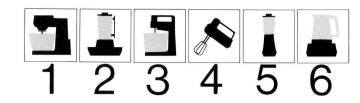

2 5 6 PINEAPPLE WHIP

For 4 portions:
1 large (15oz) can pineapple pieces
1 orange
2 standard eggs
1oz cornflour
2oz castor sugar
Glacé cherries
Angelica

1 Drain syrup from pineapple pieces and place in a measuring jug.
2 Grate rind and squeeze juice from orange and add to syrup. Make up to $\frac{1}{2}$ pint with water, if necessary.
3 Separate eggs; place yolks in liquidiser goblet and whites in a clean, grease-free bowl.
4 Add cornflour and half of the syrup to liquidiser goblet and run machine until blended. (If using large type of liquidiser, all the syrup may be added.) Place in a small saucepan with remaining syrup and bring to boil, stirring continuously; cook for 2 minutes. Leave to cool. Stir in pineapple pieces.
5 Whisk egg whites until stiff, but not dry, and whisk in half the sugar. Fold in remaining sugar, then fold into pineapple mixture. Pile into 4 glass dishes and decorate with cherries and angelica. Serve with crisp, sweet biscuits.

2 6 GAELIC CHOCOLATE WHIP

For 4 portions:
$\frac{1}{2}$oz (or 1 envelope) gelatine
3 tablespoons cold water
3 level tablespoons cocoa
3 level tablespoons castor sugar
A few drops vanilla essence
$\frac{3}{4}$ pint milk
1 standard egg
1 small can evaporated milk
1 small ($2\frac{7}{8}$ fluid oz) carton double cream
1 dessertspoon milk
2 small chocolate flake bars

1 Place gelatine in a small bowl, add water. Place cocoa, sugar, vanilla essence and $\frac{3}{4}$ pint milk in liquidiser goblet. Separate egg and add egg yolk to liquidiser; run until well mixed. Pour into a saucepan and bring to boil. Simmer for 2 minutes, stirring occasionally. Return to liquidiser and add gelatine; run machine until gelatine has melted.
2 Remove small cap from lid of liquidiser and pour in evaporated milk; run machine until well mixed. Leave

chocolate mixture in liquidiser in a cool place until partially set.
3 Whisk egg white until stiff, but not dry. When chocolate mixture is partially set, run liquidiser until mixture is light and frothy, then fold into egg white. Turn into tall individual glasses and leave to set.
4 Whisk double cream and milk together until thick, but still of pouring consistency. Pour a layer on top of each glass. Cut each flake in half and place a piece in each glass.

2 6 APRICOT DELICE

For 6 portions:
1 lemon flavour jelly
$\frac{1}{4}$ pint boiling water
1 large (15oz) can apricot halves
1 small can evaporated milk
1 small bar chocolate flake

1 Cut jelly into cubes and place in liquidiser goblet with the boiling water, and run machine until dissolved.
2 Strain syrup from apricots, make up to $\frac{1}{4}$ pint with cold water, if necessary, and add to jelly; run machine until mixed. Leave in a cool place until nearly set.
3 Add apricots and evaporated milk to liquidiser and run machine until smooth and thoroughly blended.
4 Pour into a serving dish and leave to set.
5 Decorate with crushed chocolate flake.

2 6 ORANGE DELIGHTS

For 4 portions:
1 (11oz) can mandarin oranges
1 packet orange flavour jelly
$\frac{1}{4}$ pint boiling water
1 small can evaporated milk

1 Drain mandarin oranges; make up syrup to $\frac{1}{4}$ pint with cold water.
2 Cut jelly into cubes and place in liquidiser goblet with the boiling water; run machine until dissolved. Add mandarin syrup and run machine for a few seconds. Leave in liquidiser goblet, in a cold place, to partially set.
3 When on the point of setting, switch on liquidiser, remove small cap in lid and pour in evaporated milk. Run liquidiser until frothy. Save 12 mandarin orange segments for decoration. Add remainder to liquidiser and stir with a spoon. Pour into individual glasses and leave to set. Decorate each dish with 3 mandarin orange segments.

Rhubarb and Orange Meringue

Use tender, pink, early rhubarb or fresh garden rhubarb, when in season, for this delicious meringue pudding

1 2 3 4 6

RHUBARB AND ORANGE MERINGUE

(pictured on pages 54, 55)

For 6 portions:
1lb rhubarb
1 orange
2oz granulated sugar
1oz cornflour
2 standard eggs
3oz castor sugar

1 Prepare a cool oven (325 deg F, Gas Mark 3).
2 Wash and trim rhubarb and cut into short lengths. Place in a 2-pint casserole or pie dish.
3 Grate rind and squeeze juice from orange. Place in a measuring jug and make up to $\frac{3}{4}$ pint with water.
4 Place orange juice in liquidiser goblet; add granulated sugar and cornflour and run machine until blended. Pour into a small saucepan and bring to boil, stirring, and simmer for 3 minutes; allow to cool slightly.
5 Separate eggs. Place whites in mixer bowl (clean and grease-free). Stir yolks into orange sauce; pour over rhubarb and cook in centre of oven for 20 minutes. Turn oven down to 300 deg F, Gas Mark 2.
6 Whisk egg whites until stiff and dry. Whisk in half castor sugar and whisk until stiff again. Fold in remaining sugar with a metal spoon. Spread over rhubarb mixture and return to oven to cook for a further 20 to 25 minutes until meringue is golden brown and the rhubarb tender.

1 2 3 4 5 6

OLIVER'S CHOCOLATE PUDDING

For 4 portions:
PUDDING
3oz butter or margarine
3oz castor sugar
2 standard eggs
3oz self-raising flour
1 level tablespoon cocoa

SAUCE
1oz butter or margarine
1 level dessertspoon cocoa
1 level dessertspoon instant coffee
1 level tablespoon castor sugar
1 level tablespoon cornflour
$\frac{1}{2}$ pint boiling water

Castor sugar

1 Prepare a moderate oven (375 deg F, Gas Mark 5). Grease a 2-pint pie dish.
2 Place butter, cut into pieces, and sugar, in mixer bowl;

beat until light and fluffy. Add eggs, one at a time, beating well after each addition.
3 Sift flour and cocoa together and carefully fold into creamed mixture, cutting through with a metal spoon. Spread mixture evenly in dish.
4 Place all ingredients for sauce in liquidiser goblet and run machine until well blended. Pour over pudding mixture. Place pie dish on a baking sheet.
5 Bake on second shelf from top of oven for 35 to 40 minutes. Test by pressing with fingers. If cooked, pudding should spring back and have begun to shrink from sides of dish. Dredge with castor sugar and serve hot.

2 5

CHOCOLATE MOUSSE

For each portion:
1oz plain chocolate
1 standard egg
1 dessertspoon boiling water
1 teaspoon of rum or $\frac{1}{2}$ teaspoon vanilla essence

1 Break chocolate into squares. Place in grinder and run machine until finely ground. (If using a machine without a grinder, place in liquidiser goblet.)
2 Separate egg and place yolk in liquidiser (if chocolate has been ground in liquidiser, add yolk to it) and the white in a clean, grease-free bowl. Add chocolate, boiling water and rum or vanilla essence to liquidiser and run machine until well mixed.
3 Whisk egg white until stiff, but not dry, add chocolate mixture and fold in until well blended. Pour into a sundae glass and leave in a cool place to set. Serve with cream.
NOTE: When making mousse for 3 or 4 portions in a small liquidiser, it is necessary to grind the chocolate half at a time.

2 6

LEMON MALLOW PIE

For 4 or 5 portions:
2oz butter
6oz digestive biscuits
2oz demerara sugar
1 packet lemon flavour jelly
$\frac{1}{4}$ pint boiling water
1 lemon
1 large can sweetened condensed milk
1 chocolate flake bar

1 Melt butter in a saucepan. Place biscuits, a few at a time, in liquidiser goblet and run machine until reduced to fine crumbs; place in a bowl, add demerara sugar and butter; mix well. Press into bottom and sides of an $8\frac{1}{2}$in glass pie plate.
2 Cut jelly into cubes and place in liquidiser goblet with boiling water and run machine until dissolved.

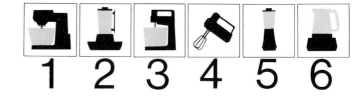

3 Thinly pare rind from lemon and add to liquidiser. Cut away pith from lemon and discard; chop flesh and place in liquidiser with jelly. Run machine for a few seconds until well mixed. Strain into a bowl, then return strained mixture to liquidiser. Add condensed milk and run machine until thoroughly mixed; pour into biscuit-crumb pie shell.
4 Decorate with chocolate flake. Leave in a cool place to set. Serve cold.

1 3 4   STEAMED JAM PUDDING

For 4 portions:
2 level tablespoons raspberry jam
4oz self-raising flour
½ level teaspoon baking powder
3oz best-quality margarine
3oz castor sugar
2 standard eggs
1 tablespoon milk

1 Prepare a steamer and put to heat. Grease a piece of greaseproof paper and a 1½-pint pudding basin. Place jam in bottom of basin.
2 Place remaining ingredients in mixer bowl, and run machine until well mixed. Place in basin and smooth top.
3 Cover with the greaseproof paper and twist securely around edge. Steam for 1½ to 2 hours.
4 Turn out on to a hot plate and serve with custard or jam sauce made by heating 3 tablespoons of jam with 1 tablespoon of water.

1 3 4 CHOCOLATE MANDARIN PUDDING

For 4 to 5 portions:
PUDDING
4oz self-raising flour
2 level teaspoons cocoa
4oz margarine
4oz castor sugar
2 standard eggs
2oz fresh white breadcrumbs
Milk to mix

CHOCOLATE SAUCE
1 (11oz) can mandarin oranges
Water
4 rounded tablespoons drinking chocolate
½oz butter
2 tablespoons milk

1 Grease a 1½-pint ring jelly mould or 1-pint pudding basin and a piece of greaseproof paper or foil to cover pudding. Prepare a steamer. Sift flour and cocoa together.

2 Place margarine, cut into pieces, and sugar, in mixer bowl and beat until light and fluffy. Add eggs, one at a time, beating well after each addition. Fold in flour and breadcrumbs and add sufficient milk to make a soft mixture.
3 Spoon into mould or basin, cover with greased greaseproof paper or foil and steam for 1½ to 2 hours.
4 To make sauce: Drain mandarin oranges, place syrup in a measuring jug and make up to ½ pint with water. Pour into a saucepan, add drinking chocolate, bring to boil, stirring, then simmer for 10 minutes. Stir in butter and milk.
5 To serve: Turn pudding on to a warm plate and decorate with mandarin orange segments. Serve hot with sauce.

1 2 3 4 5 6
LEMON MERINGUE PIE
(pictured on front cover and page 10)
For 4 to 6 portions:
SHORTCRUST PASTRY
4oz plain flour
¼ level teaspoon salt
1oz margarine, 1oz lard
Cold water to mix

FILLING
1 lemon
½ pint water
1½oz cornflour
4oz castor sugar
2 egg yolks

MERINGUE
2 egg whites
1½oz castor sugar

1 Prepare a hot oven (425 deg F, Gas Mark 7).
2 Make up shortcrust pastry according to directions on page 7. Roll out pastry and line a 7in fluted flan ring; prick well. Place a circle of greaseproof paper in flan and fill with baking beans or rice. Bake in centre of oven for 15 minutes. Remove beans and paper and return to oven for a further 5 to 10 minutes, until golden brown. Leave to cool on a wire rack. Turn oven heat to very cool (225 deg F, Gas Mark ¼).
3 Thinly pare rind from lemon and place in liquidiser goblet. Cut away white pith from lemon and discard. Cut lemon into quarters and place in liquidiser. Add water, cornflour and sugar; run machine to chop lemon. Strain into a saucepan.
4 Stir over moderate heat until sauce boils; cook, stirring for 2 minutes, cool slightly, then beat in egg yolks. Pour into flan case.
5 Place egg whites in clean, grease-free mixer bowl and whisk at high speed until stiff, but not dry. Whisk in sugar. Pile meringue on top of lemon mixture and bake until pale golden brown, about 30 minutes. Serve warm.

Orange and Coffee Pavlova

You'll find it easy to make this spectacular sweet with the help of your mixer. It can be made in advance and stored in an air-tight tin for up to two weeks. Fill and decorate it just before serving

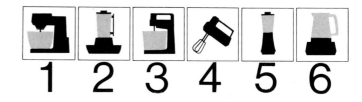

1 2 3 4 5 6

ORANGE AND COFFEE PAVLOVA
(pictured left)

For 6 portions:
PAVLOVA
3 standard eggs
1 level teaspoon cornflour
1 level dessertspoon instant coffee powder
1 teaspoon vinegar
1 teaspoon water
7oz castor sugar

FILLING
1oz cornflour
½oz sugar
1 (11oz) can mandarin oranges
Milk
1 small (2⅞ fluid oz) carton double cream

1 Prepare a cool oven (300 deg F, Gas Mark 2). Wet a baking sheet and cover with greaseproof or silicone-treated paper.
2 Prepare Pavlova: Separate eggs and place whites in clean, grease-free mixer bowl and yolks on one side for filling. Whisk egg whites until stiff, but not dry.
3 Mix cornflour, instant coffee, vinegar and water together and whisk into egg whites, with sugar, until well blended. Mixture will be heavy and smooth.
4 Spread mixture on baking sheet to an even circle, about 1in thick.
5 Place in centre of oven and immediately turn heat down to 275 deg F, Gas Mark 1. Cook for 1 hour, after which Pavlova should be crisp on outside and marshmallow-like on inside.
6 Turn oven off and leave to cool in oven without opening door.
7 Prepare filling: Place cornflour and sugar in liquidiser goblet. Drain syrup from mandarins and make up to ½ pint with milk. (It may have a curdled appearance, but this does not matter.) Add to liquidiser and run machine until well mixed. Pour into a saucepan and cook until mixture thickens and boils; cook for 2 minutes. (Sauce will have a very curdled appearance as it comes to the boil, but this will disappear as it thickens.)
8 Place egg yolks in liquidiser goblet, add sauce and run machine until well mixed. Pour into a bowl and cover with damp greaseproof paper to prevent a skin forming, and leave to become quite cold.
9 Just before serving, place Pavlova on a flat serving dish. Reserve some mandarins for decoration and place remainder in centre.
10 Whisk cream until stiff and fold into filling. Pile on top of mandarins and decorate with remaining mandarins.

4   APPLE MARSHMALLOW

For 4 portions:
1½lb cooking apples
4 tablespoons water
2 standard eggs
1 tablespoon lemon juice
3 rounded tablespoons raspberry jam, sieved
1 rounded tablespoon golden syrup

1 Peel and slice apples. Stew in a covered saucepan with the water until tender. Beat until smooth.
2 Separate eggs and place each white in a separate basin, beat yolks into apple and stir over moderate heat for 2 minutes; do not allow to boil. Remove from heat and stir in lemon juice and strawberry jam.
3 Whisk 1 egg white until stiff, but not dry. Add apple mixture and continue whisking until fluffy. Spoon into 4 individual glasses.
4 Wash and dry beaters. Add golden syrup to remaining egg white and whisk over hot water until very light and fluffy. Spoon on top of apple mixture in each glass.

1 3 4   APRICOT AND APPLE WHIRLIGIG

For 4 portions:
1 large cooking apple
4 rounded tablespoons apricot jam

SCONE DOUGH
4oz self-raising flour
Pinch of salt
1 rounded teaspoon sugar
2oz margarine
2 tablespoons milk

1 Prepare a hot oven (425 deg F, Gas Mark 7).
2 Peel, core and thinly slice apple into a shallow, round ovenproof dish. Spread with 2 tablespoons of jam. Place in centre of oven and bake for 10 minutes.
3 Place flour, salt and sugar in mixer bowl. Cut margarine into pieces, add to flour and run machine until mixture resembles fine breadcrumbs. Add milk and mix with a fork to make a firm dough.
4 Roll out scone dough on a floured board to an oblong, 8in by 6in. Spread with 2 rounded tablespoonsful of jam and roll up, from the long side, like a Swiss roll. Cut into 8 (1in) pieces.
5 Remove dish from oven and place scones around edge of dish, leaving a small space between each. Return dish to oven and bake for a further 15 minutes. Serve hot with custard or cream.

59

2 6   BANANA CARAMEL CUSTARD

For 4 portions:
3 large or 4 standard eggs
$\frac{3}{4}$ pint milk
$\frac{1}{2}$oz castor sugar
2oz granulated sugar
2 tablespoons water
3 bananas
A little whipped cream
A few browned and shredded almonds

1   Prepare a very cool oven (275 deg F, Gas Mark 1). Half fill a roasting tin with warm water.
2   Place eggs, milk and castor sugar in liquidiser goblet and run machine until blended.
3   Place granulated sugar and water in a thick saucepan and heat slowly until sugar has dissolved; boil steadily, without stirring, until sugar turns a deep golden brown.
4   Run liquidiser at lowest speed and add caramel, a little at a time, until thoroughly blended. Pour into a $1\frac{1}{4}$-pint soufflé dish. Place dish in water bath and place in centre of oven; cook for $1\frac{1}{4}$ hours or until set. Remove dish from roasting tin and leave until custard is quite cold (about 3 hours).
5   Loosen edge by pulling towards centre gently with fingers, and turn out on to a serving dish.
6   Peel and slice bananas and place a border around edge of serving dish. Pipe a few rosettes of cream on top of custard and sprinkle them with browned and shredded almonds. Decorate top with remaining slices of banana.

1 3 4   ROSY PEACH MACAROONS

For 8 portions:
$1\frac{1}{2}$oz ground almonds
2oz semolina
4oz castor sugar
2 standard egg whites
$\frac{1}{2}$ teaspoon almond essence
4 fresh peaches
$\frac{3}{4}$ pint water
4oz granulated sugar
1 level tablespoon cornflour
Pink food colouring
1 small ($2\frac{7}{8}$ fluid oz) carton double cream

1   Prepare a moderate oven (350 deg F, Gas Mark 4). Line 2 baking sheets with rice paper or silicone-treated baking paper.
2   Mix together almonds, semolina and castor sugar. Place egg whites in clean, grease-free mixer bowl and whisk until stiff, but not dry. Beat in almond essence. Fold almond mixture into egg whites.

3   Pipe or spoon 4 heaps of almond mixture, each about $1\frac{1}{2}$in in diameter, on to each baking sheet, leaving plenty of space between them.
4   Bake in centre of oven for 20 to 25 minutes, until lightly browned and firm, but not hard. Place on a wire rack to cool.
5   Halve peaches and carefully remove stones. Place the water and granulated sugar in a frying pan or shallow saucepan and heat gently until sugar is dissolved. Place peach halves in this syrup and poach gently for 10 to 15 minutes until peach skins can be peeled off easily. Remove peaches from pan and drain on kitchen paper; peel off skins.
6   Boil syrup quickly for about 10 minutes until it is reduced to $\frac{1}{2}$ pint. Blend cornflour with a little cold water; add to syrup and bring to boil, stirring. Cook for 3 minutes, stirring continuously. Tint pink with colouring. Allow to cool.
7   Just before serving, place a drained peach half, rounded side uppermost, on each macaroon. Whisk cream until stiff. Pipe or spoon a swirl of cream on each peach half; arrange on large serving dish. Spoon a little syrup over cream; serve any remaining syrup separately.
NOTE: Macaroons can be made up to a week in advance and stored in an air-tight container until required.

1 3 4   SPICED PEAR TOPSY TURVY

For 4 portions:
TOPPING
1oz best-quality margarine
1oz soft brown sugar
1 large ($15\frac{1}{2}$oz) can pear halves, drained

PUDDING
4oz self-raising flour
1 level teaspoon baking powder
2 level teaspoons cinnamon
4oz best-quality margarine
4oz soft brown sugar
2 standard eggs

1   Prepare a cool oven (325 deg F, Gas Mark 3). Grease a 7in square shallow tin and line the base with a piece of greaseproof paper; grease paper.
2   To make topping: Cream margarine and sugar together and spread on base of tin. Arrange pears, cut sides downwards, radiating from centre, on top.
3   To make pudding: Place all pudding ingredients into mixer bowl and run machine for 1 to 2 minutes until well mixed. Spread over pears; smooth top carefully.
4   Bake in centre of oven for 40 to 45 minutes until well risen and golden brown.
5   Invert on to a warm serving dish and serve immediately.

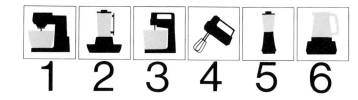

1 3 CRISPY PLUM PIE

For 4 portions:
1lb plums

SHORTCRUST PASTRY
6oz plain flour
$\frac{1}{4}$ level teaspoon salt
1$\frac{1}{2}$oz margarine
1$\frac{1}{2}$oz lard
Cold water to mix

CRUMBLE
1$\frac{1}{2}$oz plain flour
5oz to 7oz castor sugar
2oz margarine

1 Prepare a moderately hot oven (400 deg F, Gas Mark 6).
2 Wash and halve plums; remove stones.
3 Make shortcrust pastry, following directions on page 7.
4 Roll out pastry and line a 1$\frac{1}{2}$-pint pie dish.
5 To make crumble: Place flour and sugar in mixer bowl. Add margarine, cut into pieces, and run machine until mixture resembles fine breadcrumbs.
6 Sprinkle half the crumble over pastry base. Place plum halves on top, rounded side uppermost, and sprinkle with remaining crumble.
7 Bake in centre of oven for 30 minutes until crumble is crisp and golden. Serve hot with custard or cream.
NOTE: When plums are not in season, use gooseberries, blackcurrants or fresh apricots.

1 2 3 4 5 6 SNOW QUEENS

For 4 portions:
2oz white bread, with crusts removed
Grated rind of 1 lemon
$\frac{1}{2}$oz butter or margarine
4$\frac{1}{2}$oz castor sugar
$\frac{1}{2}$ pint milk
2 standard eggs
4 level tablespoons raspberry jam

1 Prepare a moderate oven (375 deg F, Gas Mark 5). Grease 4 individual ovenproof glass dishes.
2 Break bread into small pieces and place in liquidiser goblet, a little at a time; run machine until crumbed. Add lemon rind, butter and $\frac{1}{2}$oz castor sugar.
3 Heat milk and pour on to breadcrumbs; leave for 15 minutes.
4 Separate eggs, placing whites in clean, grease-free mixer bowl, add yolks to breadcrumb mixture and run machine until mixed. Divide evenly between ovenproof dishes.
5 Place dishes on a baking sheet in centre of oven and bake for 20 minutes until mixture is set.

6 Remove from oven and spread 1 level tablespoonful of jam over each pudding.
7 Whisk egg whites until stiff, but not dry; add half remaining sugar and whisk until stiff again. Fold in remainder with a metal spoon.
8 Place meringue in a piping bag fitted with a large star tube and pipe rosettes around edges of dishes.
9 Return to oven for a further 5 minutes until meringue tips are golden brown.

2 5 6 FIGGY PUDDING

For 4 portions:
5oz dried figs
3oz plain flour
1$\frac{1}{2}$ level teaspoons bicarbonate of soda
4oz shredded suet
3oz fresh white breadcrumbs
3oz demerara sugar
2oz raisins
Grated rind of 1 lemon
2 standard eggs
1 level tablespoon golden syrup
1 level tablespoon black treacle
$\frac{1}{2}$ pint milk
1 dessertspoon lemon juice

1 Grease a 2-pint pudding basin and a piece of greaseproof paper to cover pudding. Prepare a steamer. Wash and dry figs, then chop roughly.
2 Sift flour and bicarbonate of soda into a bowl; stir in suet, breadcrumbs, sugar, figs, raisins and lemon rind.
3 Place eggs, syrup, treacle, milk and lemon juice in liquidiser goblet and run machine until well mixed. Add to dry ingredients and mix well.
4 Turn mixture into pudding basin, cover with greaseproof paper and twist paper around edge. Steam for 1$\frac{1}{2}$ to 2 hours.
5 Serve pudding hot with warmed golden syrup or custard.

4 ZABAGLIONE

For each portion:
1 egg yolk
1 rounded teaspoon castor sugar
1 tablespoon sherry

1 Place a deep bowl over a saucepan of hot, but not boiling water.
2 Add the egg yolk, sugar and sherry and whisk until mixture has trebled in bulk. Pour into a small glass and serve immediately with crisp, sweet biscuits.
NOTE: Fresh orange juice can be substituted for sherry, but add a large pinch of grated orange rind for each person.

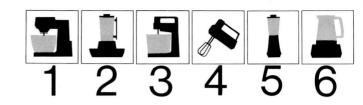

1 2 3 4 5 6

1 3 4   SPANISH ANGEL PIE

For 4 to 6 portions:
MERINGUE CASE
2oz walnuts
2 standard egg whites
$\frac{1}{4}$ level teaspoon salt
$\frac{1}{4}$ level teaspoon cream of tartar
4oz castor sugar
$\frac{1}{4}$ teaspoon vanilla essence

FILLING
1$\frac{1}{2}$oz plain chocolate
$\frac{1}{2}$ level teaspoon instant coffee powder
1 teaspoon water
1 (5 fluid oz) carton double cream

1 Prepare a very cool oven (275 deg F, Gas Mark 1).
Grease an 8$\frac{1}{2}$in ovenproof pie plate with butter.
Chop walnuts.
2 Place egg whites in clean, grease-free mixer bowl; run machine until whites are foamy. Add salt and cream of tartar. Continue whisking until mixture stands in stiff peaks. Add sugar gradually, whisking continuously, until mixture again stands in peaks.
3 Fold in nuts and vanilla essence. Turn into pie plate; spread mixture to sides to form a pie case. Bake in centre of oven until firm and lightly browned, about 45 minutes. Leave to cool.
4 To make filling: Break up chocolate, and place in a basin with coffee and water over a small pan of hot water. Leave until chocolate is melted. Stir and cool slightly.
5 Whip cream; fold in chocolate mixture. Pour into cold meringue case and spread right to edges. Chill in refrigerator for at least 4 hours. Cut in wedges to serve.

1 3 4   BANANA AND CHERRY WHIP

For 6 portions:
1 pint milk
2oz semolina
2 rounded tablespoons granulated sugar
1 packet lemon flavour jelly
2 standard eggs
1oz glacé cherries
3 bananas
Lemon juice

1 Lightly grease a deep, 7$\frac{1}{2}$in round cake tin (not loose-based).
2 Pour milk into a saucepan and place over medium heat to warm. Stir in semolina and bring to boil, stirring. Reduce

heat to low and cook for 7 minutes, stirring continuously with a wooden spoon. Remove from heat. Add sugar and jelly and stir until dissolved.
3 Separate eggs. Place whites in clean, grease-free mixer bowl and beat yolks into semolina. Allow to cool.
4 Chop cherries. Peel and chop 2 bananas. Whisk egg whites until stiff, but not dry.
5 Whisk semolina with a fork until creamy. Stir in cherries and bananas and lightly fold in whisked egg white, using a metal spoon.
6 Pour into cake tin and leave in a cool place for 3 to 4 hours, until set.
7 Peel and slice remaining banana and toss in lemon juice to prevent browning. Turn out whip, and decorate with banana slices.

2 5 6   ORANGE CARAMEL PUDDING
(pictured right)

For 4 to 6 portions:
1 heaped tablespoon golden syrup
2 oranges
3oz fresh white bread, with crusts removed
3oz plain flour
1 rounded teaspoon baking powder
3oz shredded suet
2oz castor sugar
1 standard egg
Milk to mix

1 Prepare a steamer and put to heat. Grease a double sheet of greaseproof paper or a piece of foil to cover.
2 Place golden syrup in a saucepan and heat until a deep caramel colour. Quickly coat the inside of a 1$\frac{1}{2}$-pint pudding basin.
3 Grate rind from oranges and set aside for pudding. Remove peel and pith from orange and discard; cut orange into thin slices, then line basin with them, over caramel.
4 Break bread into pieces and place in liquidiser goblet and run machine until finely crumbed. Place in a bowl. Add flour, baking powder, suet, sugar and orange rind and mix well.
5 Mix to a soft dropping consistency with egg and milk.
6 Put mixture in basin and cover with greased greaseproof paper or foil, making a pleat to allow for rising. Tie down securely.
7 Steam for 1$\frac{1}{2}$ hours, replacing water in steamer, if necessary.
8 Turn out on to a warm plate and serve with a jug of warm syrup.

Orange Caramel Pudding

The family will love this pudding on a cold, frosty day. The secret of its light texture is the added breadcrumbs in the mixture; these can be made quickly in your liquidiser

1 3 4 APPLE AND RASPBERRY BAKE

For 4 portions:
2 cooking apples
1oz best-quality margarine
4oz plain flour
$\frac{1}{4}$ level teaspoon salt
2 level teaspoons baking powder
2oz castor sugar
6 tablespoons milk
4 level tablespoons raspberry jam
$\frac{1}{4}$ pint water

1 Prepare a moderate oven (375 deg F, Gas Mark 5).
Grease a shallow 2$\frac{1}{2}$-pint ovenproof dish.
2 Peel, core and slice apples into dish.
3 Place margarine, cut into small pieces, flour, salt, baking
powder, sugar and milk in mixer bowl; run machine until
smooth. Spread mixture over apple slices.
4 Put jam and water into a small saucepan and bring
slowly to boil, stirring continuously. Pour over
pudding mixture.
5 Place on a baking sheet and bake in centre of oven for 45
minutes. The jam sauce will seep through and the sponge
should be golden brown. Serve hot with custard or cream.

1 3 4 DATE AND LEMON PUDDING

For 4 portions:
6oz self-raising flour
3oz margarine
3oz castor sugar
Rind of 1 small lemon
4oz cooking dates
1 standard egg
$\frac{1}{4}$ pint milk

1 Prepare a moderate oven (350 deg F, Gas Mark 4).
Grease a 1$\frac{1}{2}$-pint ovenproof dish.
2 Place flour in mixer bowl. Add margarine, cut into pieces.
Run machine until mixture resembles fine breadcrumbs. Stir
in sugar. Grate rind of lemon and add to mixture. Roughly
chop dates and add, with egg and milk; mix well. Turn into
prepared dish.
3 Bake in the centre of oven for about 1 hour until risen and
golden brown. Serve hot with custard.

1 3 4 CRUNCHY FRUIT CRUMBLE

For 4 portions:
1lb fruit (apples, plums or rhubarb)
1 tablespoon water
1 level tablespoon castor sugar

TOPPING
4oz plain flour
2oz margarine
3oz demerara sugar
2oz fresh white breadcrumbs
$\frac{1}{2}$oz butter

1 Prepare a moderate oven (350 deg F, Gas Mark 4).
2 Prepare fruit in the usual way and place in a 1-pint
ovenproof dish. Sprinkle with water and castor sugar.
3 Place flour in mixer bowl. Add margarine, cut into small
pieces, and run machine until mixture resembles fine
breadcrumbs. Add demerara sugar and mix well.
4 Place in a layer over fruit. Cover with a layer of breadcrumbs and dot with butter.
5 Place on a baking sheet in the centre of oven and cook
for about 1 hour. Serve hot with custard or cream.

1 3 4 HONEY SNOW

For 4 portions:
2 standard eggs
3 level tablespoons clear honey
2oz marshmallows
1oz cornflour
$\frac{1}{2}$ pint milk
1 tablespoon orange squash
1 tablespoon lemon juice
2oz plain chocolate

1 Separate eggs. Place whites in mixer bowl (clean and
grease free). Mix yolks and honey together in a basin. Chop
marshmallows roughly.
2 Mix cornflour with a little of the measured milk. Put
remainder of milk on to heat. Pour over mixed cornflour,
return to pan and bring to boil, stirring. Cook for 3 minutes,
stirring continuously. Reduce heat, add honey mixture and
marshmallows and stir until marshmallows have melted.
3 Remove from heat and stir in fruit juices. Leave to cool,
stirring occasionally.
4 Whisk egg whites stiffly and fold into cooked mixture.
Pile into 4 individual glasses. Grate chocolate and sprinkle
on top of each portion.

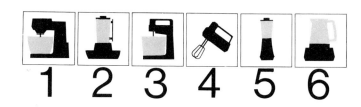

1 3 4 6   SPICY APPLE BARS

For 6 portions:
6oz plain flour
½ level teaspoon salt
3oz margarine
3oz moist brown sugar

TOPPING
1 rounded tablespoon castor sugar
1 level teaspoon cinnamon
2 cooking apples
1oz butter

1 Prepare a moderately hot oven (400 deg F, Gas Mark 6).
2 Place flour and salt into mixer bowl, add margarine, cut into pieces, and run machine until mixture resembles fine breadcrumbs. Stir in moist brown sugar and spread in a 7in shallow, square tin.
3 Mix together castor sugar and cinnamon in a small basin.
4 Peel, core and slice apples; arrange over mixture in the tin. Sprinkle with sugar and cinnamon and dot with butter.
5 Place on a baking sheet and bake in centre of oven for 30 minutes.
6 Cut into 6 bars and serve hot or cold with cream, ice cream or custard.

2 5 6   RASPBERRY WATER ICE

For 4 portions:
¼ pint water
2oz sugar
½lb raspberries

1 Turn refrigerator to coldest setting.
2 Place water and sugar in a saucepan and bring to boil, stirring, until sugar has dissolved. Remove from heat and leave to cool.
3 Wash raspberries and drain well. Place in liquidiser goblet and run machine until raspberries are broken down; strain.
4 Mix syrup and purée, and pour into a freezing tray or plastic tray and leave in ice-making compartment of refrigerator for 1½ hours.
5 Remove mixture from refrigerator, scrape into a bowl and whisk until smooth. Return to tray and freeze for at least 1 hour. Turn refrigerator back to normal setting.
6 Serve with crisp sugar wafers.
NOTE: This is a very rich sweet, and only a small portion should be served.

1 3 4   BAKEWELL TART

For 4 to 6 portions:
SHORTCRUST PASTRY
4oz plain flour
1oz margarine
1oz cooking fat
Cold water to mix

FILLING
2oz castor sugar
2oz butter, softened
1 standard egg
½ teaspoon almond essence
2oz self-raising flour
3 level tablespoons raspberry jam

ICING
1oz flaked almonds
4oz icing sugar
1 to 2 tablespoons hot water

1 Prepare a moderate oven (350 deg F, Gas Mark 4).
2 Make Shortcrust Pastry, following directions for basic recipe on page 7.
3 Roll out pastry and line a 7¾in by 1¼in deep pie tin, leaving enough to decorate rim. Cut edge with back of knife to form flakes. Brush rim with water.
4 Roll out remaining pastry and cut small circles, using a ½in plain piping tube or thimble. Arrange along pastry rim, slightly overlapping, and press down lightly.
5 Place sugar, butter, egg, almond essence and flour in mixer bowl. Run machine until well mixed.
6 Spread jam in bottom of pastry case and cover with filling mixture. Smooth with back of a spoon.
7 Place on a baking sheet and bake just above centre of oven for 30 to 35 minutes, until golden brown and firm to the touch. Leave in tin until cold, then transfer to a serving dish.
8 Brown almonds under a medium grill. Sieve icing sugar into a basin and stir in sufficient hot water to make a thick icing. Spread over filling and sprinkle with browned almonds.

Cakes and Biscuits

Frosted Chocolate Gâteau
Top this rich, dark chocolate cake with a delicious, 'gooey' frosting, which can be quickly whipped up in a mixer

For melt-in-the-mouth cakes and biscuits without effort, a mixer is a must. The liquidiser, too, can be used for making cakes. If you have only a small mixer or hand whisk, let the mixer do the hard work of creaming, whisking or rubbing in; do the rest by hand.

1 2 3 4 5 6

1 3 4   MADEIRA CAKE

6oz best-quality margarine
6oz castor sugar
Grated rind of half a lemon
3 standard eggs
8oz plain flour
1½ level teaspoons baking powder
2 tablespoons milk
Thin strip candied citron peel (optional)

1 Prepare a cool oven (325 deg F, Gas Mark 3). Grease a deep, round, 7in cake tin and line with a double thickness of greaseproof paper; brush paper with oil or melted fat.
2 Place margarine, cut into pieces, and sugar, with lemon rind, in mixer bowl and cream together until light and fluffy.
3 Beat in eggs, one at a time, beating well after each addition. Fold in flour, baking powder and milk, cutting through with a metal spoon.
4 Place in tin, smooth top and arrange citron peel in centre.
5 Bake cake in centre of oven for 1½ hours. Test by pressing with fingers. If cooked, cake should spring back, have stopped bubbling and have begun to shrink from sides of tin. Turn out, remove paper and leave to cool on a wire rack.

1 3 4   FROSTED CHOCOLATE GATEAU
(pictured left)

4oz best-quality margarine
4oz castor sugar
3oz self-raising flour
1oz cocoa
1 level teaspoon baking powder
2 standard eggs
2 tablespoons milk

BUTTER ICING
2oz butter
6oz icing sugar
2 tablespoons orange juice
2 level teaspoons grated orange rind

FROSTING
American Frosting or Jiffy American Frosting
  (see page 9)

DECORATION
Orange jelly sweets
Block chocolate

1 Prepare a cool oven (325 deg F, Gas Mark 3). Brush 2 (7in) sandwich tins with oil or melted fat and line each with a circle of greaseproof paper, then grease paper.

2 Cut margarine in pieces and place, with other cake ingredients, in mixer bowl; run machine for 1 to 2 minutes until smooth and well mixed. Divide mixture evenly between tins and smooth surface.
3 Bake cakes in centre of oven for about 35 minutes. Test by pressing with fingers. If cooked, cakes should spring back, have stopped bubbling and have begun to shrink from sides of tin. Turn out, remove paper and leave to cool on a wire rack.
4 Prepare butter icing as directed on page 9, using ingredients listed above, and use to sandwich cakes together. Prepare either American Frosting or Jiffy American Frosting, as directed on page 9.
5 Place cake on a plate, quickly spread frosting over cake and make peaks with a round-bladed knife. Leave to set. Decorate with orange jelly sweets and chocolate curls, made by cutting shavings of block chocolate with a potato peeler.

1 3 4   DUNDEE CAKE

4oz whole almonds
8oz currants
8oz sultanas
8oz seedless raisins
2oz glacé cherries
4oz mixed cut peel
1 lemon
8oz butter or margarine
8oz castor sugar
4 standard eggs
12oz plain flour
1 level teaspoon mixed spice

1 Prepare a very cool oven (275 deg F, Gas Mark 1). Grease a deep, round 8in cake tin and line with a double thickness of greaseproof paper; brush paper with oil or melted fat.
2 Blanch almonds, wash and dry fruit, if necessary, quarter cherries and grate rind and squeeze juice of lemon.
3 Place butter, cut into pieces, and sugar in mixer bowl and cream together until light and fluffy. Add eggs, one at a time, beating well after each addition. Mix in fruit and lemon rind.
4 Add flour, spice and lemon juice to mixture. Run machine at low speed until well mixed.
5 Spread in tin and level off with fork. Arrange almonds on top.
6 Bake in centre of oven for 4 to 4½ hours. Test by pressing with fingers. If cooked, cake should spring back, have stopped bubbling and have begun to shrink from sides of tin. Leave to cool in tin. Remove paper, wrap in greaseproof paper and store in an air-tight tin.
NOTE: This cake improves with keeping.

1 HONEY FUDGE CAKE

6oz best-quality margarine
6oz castor sugar
1 level tablespoon clear honey
3 standard eggs
8oz self-raising flour
1 level teaspoon baking powder
5 tablespoons milk
1 teaspoon almond essence

LEMON BUTTER ICING
4oz butter
8oz icing sugar
1 lemon

FUDGE ICING
12oz icing sugar
4oz margarine
1 level tablespoon clear honey
2 tablespoons milk

Toasted flaked almonds for decoration

1 Prepare a moderate oven (375 deg F, Gas Mark 5). Brush 3 (8in) sandwich tins with oil or melted fat and line each with a circle of greaseproof paper; grease paper.
2 Place margarine, cut into pieces, and all other cake ingredients in mixer bowl and run machine for 1 to 2 minutes until smooth and well mixed. Divide mixture evenly between prepared tins, and smooth surfaces.
3 Bake in centre of oven for 18 to 20 minutes. Test by pressing with fingers. If cooked, cakes should spring back, have stopped bubbling and have begun to shrink from sides of tins. Turn out, remove paper and leave to cool on wire racks.
4 Place butter, cut into pieces, and icing sugar, in mixer bowl and run machine until mixture is light and fluffy. Grate lemon rind finely and squeeze juice. Beat rind and 2 tablespoonsful of juice carefully into butter icing.
5 When cakes are completely cooled, sandwich the 3 layers together with lemon butter icing and place on a plate.
6 To make fudge icing: Place icing sugar in mixer bowl. Cut margarine into pieces and place in a small saucepan, with honey and milk. Heat gently until margarine has melted, then bring nearly to boil. Pour on to icing sugar and mix well. Beat until mixture has thickened sufficiently to leave a good trail.
7 Pile fudge icing on to cake and allow to spread down sides, smoothing with a knife, if necessary. Mark all over in swirls with blade of knife or back of teaspoon. Leave to become firm.
8 Decorate top with toasted flaked almonds.

1 3 4 CRUNCHY TOPPED SQUARES

Makes 15:
TOPPING
2oz glacé cherries
3oz rolled oats
3oz desiccated coconut
2oz demerara sugar
3oz margarine
2 level tablespoons golden syrup

CAKE
4oz butter or margarine
4oz castor sugar
2 standard eggs
4oz self-raising flour

1 Prepare a moderate oven (350 deg F, Gas Mark 4). Brush a shallow, 10in by 7in oblong tin with oil or melted fat and line base with greaseproof paper; grease paper.
2 To make topping: Coarsely chop cherries. Place in a bowl with oats, coconut and demerara sugar; mix well.
3 Place margarine and golden syrup in a saucepan and melt over a low heat. Pour over ingredients in bowl and stir until thoroughly mixed.
4 To make cake: Place butter, cut into pieces, and sugar, together in mixer bowl and cream until light and fluffy. Add eggs, one at a time, beating well after each addition.
5 Sift flour and fold into creamed mixture, to make a soft dropping consistency.
6 Spread mixture evenly in tin and spread topping over. Place in centre of oven and bake for 50 minutes.
Test by pressing with fingers. If cooked, cake should spring back, have stopped bubbling, and have begun to shrink from sides of tin. Allow to cool in tin before cutting into squares.

1 3 4 6 SHORTBREAD

Makes 12 biscuits:
6oz plain flour
2oz icing sugar
4oz butter

1 Prepare a moderate oven (350 deg F, Gas Mark 4).
2 Place flour and icing sugar in mixer bowl. Add butter, cut into small pieces, and run machine until mixture resembles coarse breadcrumbs.
3 Sprinkle over base of a shallow, 7in square tin. Bake in centre of oven for 30 to 35 minutes until a pale golden brown.
4 Sprinkle with castor or icing sugar, then cut into 12 fingers, and leave to cool in tin.

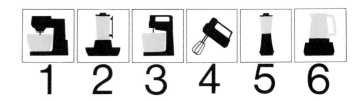

1 3 4   CALIFORNIAN CREAM SLICE
(pictured on page 70 and on front cover)

3 standard eggs
3oz castor sugar
3oz plain flour
½ level teaspoon baking powder
1oz desiccated coconut
1 large (16oz) can fruit cocktail
2 rounded teaspoons cornflour
1 (5 fluid oz) carton double cream
1 tablespoon milk
2 rounded tablespoons lemon curd

1 Prepare a moderately hot oven (400 deg F, Gas Mark 6).
Draw around base of a 12½in by 8½in Swiss-roll tin on
greaseproof paper. Cut paper ½in out from line; crease paper
on line. Brush tin with oil or melted fat; press paper into tin
and grease paper.
2 Place eggs and sugar together in a bowl and whisk at
high speed over a saucepan of hot water on the table until
mixture leaves a trail when mixer is switched off and lifted.
Remove bowl from pan and continue whisking until cool.
(If using mixer with stand and bowl, fill bowl with very hot
water, leave for a few minutes, then pour out water and
thoroughly dry bowl. Put eggs and sugar in bowl and whisk
at high speed until mixture is thick and cool.)
3 Sift flour and baking powder together, then carefully
fold into egg mixture with a metal spoon.
4 Pour into prepared tin and shake gently to level mixture.
Bake for 8 to 10 minutes in centre of oven.
5 Test by pressing with fingers. If cooked, cake should
spring back, have stopped bubbling, and have begun to
shrink from sides of tin. Cool in tin for 1 to 2 minutes. Turn
out, remove paper and cool on a wire rack. Lightly brown
coconut in residual heat of oven.
6 Drain fruit cocktail. Blend cornflour to a smooth paste
with a little of the syrup in a small saucepan; stir in remaining
syrup. Stir over a moderate heat until sauce boils; cook for 3
minutes. Stir in fruit cocktail and leave to cool.
7 Whisk cream and milk together until stiff. Fold 1 rounded
tablespoonful of whipped cream into lemon curd. Place
remaining cream in a piping bag fitted with a large star tube.
8 Trim edges of cake and cut into halves, lengthwise.
Sandwich halves together with some of lemon and cream
mixture. Spread long sides with remaining lemon cream and
press browned coconut to sides.
9 Pipe a coil of cream along each long side of top of cake
and pile fruit cocktail down centre.

1 3 4   QUICKIE FRUIT CAKE
(pictured on page 71)

6oz best-quality margarine
6oz castor sugar
3 standard eggs
4 tablespoons milk
6oz mixed currants, sultanas and raisins
2oz glacé cherries
12oz self-raising flour
1 level teaspoon mixed spice

1 Prepare a moderate oven (350 deg F, Gas Mark 4).
Brush a deep round 8in cake tin with oil or melted fat; line
with a double thickness of greaseproof paper; grease paper.
2 Place margarine, cut into pieces, with other ingredients in
mixer bowl; run machine at low speed until well mixed.
3 Place mixture in tin and smooth top with back of a
wet spoon.
4 Bake in centre of oven for 1¼ to 1½ hours. Test by pressing
with fingers. If cooked, cake should spring back, have
stopped bubbling and have begun to shrink from sides of
tin. Leave to cool in tin for 15 minutes, then turn out, remove
paper and cool on a wire rack. Store in an air-tight tin.

1 3 4   HONEY TEA LOAF
(pictured on page 71)

8oz mixed currants, sultanas and seedless raisins
¼ pint cold tea
4 level tablespoons clear honey
1 tablespoon water
1 standard egg
8oz self-raising flour
Honey to glaze

1 Place mixed dried fruit in bowl of mixer. Mix tea, honey
and water together and pour over fruit. Leave to soak
overnight.
2 Prepare a moderate oven (350 deg F, Gas Mark 4).
Grease a small loaf tin.
3 Add egg and flour to mixer bowl and mix at a low
speed. Turn into prepared tin and cook in centre of oven
for 1 to 1¼ hours, until firm and browned.
4 Leave to cool in tin for 10 minutes, then turn on to a
wire cooling rack. Brush top with honey, to form a sticky
glaze. Serve loaf sliced and buttered.
NOTE: This loaf will improve in flavour if stored for up to
4 weeks in an air-tight tin.

With a mixer, tea-time cakes are fun to make. Pictured here, from the left: Chocolate Shells, Californian Cream Slice, American Doughnuts, Quickie Fruit Cake, Coffee Nut Gâteau and Honey Tea Loaf

1 3 4 6   AMERICAN DOUGHNUTS
(pictured on page 70)

Makes about 9:
Lard or oil for deep frying
6oz self-raising flour
4oz castor sugar
2oz margarine
1 standard egg
3 tablespoons milk
1 level teaspoon cinnamon

1 Place lard in deep fat pan and heat slowly to 370 deg F (or until a small piece of day-old bread will brown in 40 seconds).
2 Place flour and 2oz of sugar in mixer bowl; add margarine, cut into small pieces. Switch on mixer to low speed and run machine until mixture resembles fine breadcrumbs. Beat egg and milk together and add to bowl. Mix to form stiff dough with fork.
3 Knead lightly on floured board, then roll out to about $\frac{1}{4}$in thickness. Cut into rounds with a plain $2\frac{3}{4}$in cutter. With a $1\frac{1}{4}$in cutter, remove a round from centre of each, to form a ring. (Cook centres separately, to make little doughnuts.)
4 Fry doughnuts in hot fat until risen and golden brown on both sides, about 2 minutes. Drain on kitchen paper.
5 Mix remaining sugar and cinnamon in a paper bag, shake 2 or 3 doughnuts at a time in bag, to coat. Serve warm or cold.

1 3 4   CHOCOLATE SHELLS
(pictured on page 70)

Makes 18 filled biscuits:
8oz butter or margarine
2oz castor sugar
$\frac{1}{2}$ teaspoon vanilla essence
7$\frac{1}{2}$oz plain flour
$\frac{1}{2}$oz cocoa

BUTTER ICING
3oz butter
6oz icing sugar

1 Prepare a moderate oven (350 deg F, Gas Mark 4). Grease 2 baking sheets.
2 Place butter, cut into pieces, and castor sugar, in mixer bowl and cream together until light and fluffy; add vanilla essence.
3 Add flour and cocoa to creamed mixture; run machine until well mixed and smooth.
4 Place mixture in a piping bag fitted with large star tube. Pipe into 36 shell shapes on baking sheets, leaving a small space between each.

5 Bake in centre of oven for 15 to 20 minutes. Leave on baking sheets for a few minutes, then place on cooling rack.
6 To make butter icing: Place butter, cut into pieces, and icing sugar in mixer bowl and cream together until light and fluffy, adding a little milk, if necessary, to give a spreading consistency.
7 Pipe or spread shells with butter icing and sandwich together. Dredge shells with icing sugar.

1 3 4   COFFEE NUT GATEAU
(pictured on page 71 and front cover)

6oz best-quality margarine
6oz castor sugar
3 standard eggs
6oz self-raising flour
1 tablespoon milk

COFFEE BUTTER ICING
6oz butter
14oz icing sugar
3 to 4 tablespoons cold, strong black coffee

2oz flaked almonds

GLACE ICING
4oz icing sugar
1 to 2 tablespoons cold, strong black coffee

Hazelnuts

1 Prepare a moderate oven (375 deg F, Gas Mark 5). Brush 2 (7$\frac{1}{2}$in) sandwich tins with oil or melted fat, line each with a circle of greaseproof paper, then grease paper.
2 Place margarine, cut into pieces, and sugar, in mixer bowl; cream together until light and fluffy. Add eggs, one at a time, beating well after each addition. Lightly fold in flour and milk, cutting through with a metal spoon. Divide mixture between tins and smooth tops.
3 Bake in centre of oven for 20 to 25 minutes, until risen and golden brown. Test by pressing with fingers. If cooked, cakes should spring back, have stopped bubbling and have begun to shrink from sides of tin. Turn out, remove paper and leave to cool on a wire rack.
4 Make up butter icing, as directed in basic recipe on page 9.
5 When cool, split each cake in half and sandwich all together with 3 layers of coffee butter icing, using about two-thirds of the icing.
6 Brown almonds under grill or in oven. Leave to cool on a sheet of greaseproof paper.

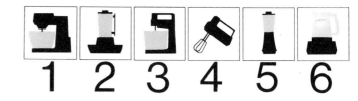

1 2 3 4 5 6

7 Spread sides of cake with half of remaining coffee butter icing. Hold bottom and top of cake in hands and dip sides into browned almonds.

8 Place cake on an 8in to 9in flat plate or cake board. Chill, if possible. Make glacé icing, as directed in basic recipe on page 9.

9 Quickly spread glacé icing over top of cake and leave in a cool place to set.

10 Fold a 9in triangle of greaseproof paper into a cone shape, secure top to prevent slipping and cut a small piece from bottom. Drop in a small, star piping tube and fill with remainder of butter icing. Fold down top of bag, to close. Pipe shells around top and bottom edges of cake and small swirls on top, over glacé icing. Top each swirl with a hazelnut.

11 Keep cake in a cool place until required.
NOTE: Cake can be made up to a week in advance and stored in an air-tight tin. Decorate just before serving.

---

1 3 4   CHOCOLATE CRISPS

Makes about 20:
4oz butter
2oz castor sugar
5oz self-raising flour
1oz drinking chocolate
Pinch of salt

1 Prepare a moderate oven (375 deg F, Gas Mark 5). Grease 2 baking sheets.

2 Place butter, cut into pieces, and sugar, in mixer bowl and run machine until mixture is light and fluffy.

3 Add remaining ingredients and run machine until just mixed.

4 Shape mixture into small balls and place on baking sheets, well apart, and flatten with fingers.

5 Bake in centre of oven for 7 to 8 minutes until just set; leave to cool for 5 minutes on baking sheet before transferring to a wire rack.

---

1 3 4 6   APRICOT AND PRUNE LOAF

4oz dried apricots
4oz prunes
2 standard eggs
8oz self-raising flour
$\frac{1}{2}$ level teaspoon salt
6oz margarine
4oz castor sugar
2 tablespoons milk

1 Prepare a moderate oven (350 deg F, Gas Mark 4). Grease and line a medium-sized, $2\frac{1}{4}$-pint loaf tin with

greaseproof paper. Brush with oil or melted fat.

2 Place apricots and prunes in a bowl, cover with boiling water and leave for 10 minutes; drain, then remove stones from prunes. Cut 3 apricots and 3 prunes in halves; keep 5 pieces of each and chop remainder.

3 Beat eggs. Sift flour and salt into mixer bowl; add margarine, cut into pieces, and run machine until mixture resembles fine breadcrumbs (do not overmix). Add sugar, chopped apricots and prunes, and mix well.

4 Add egg and milk and mix lightly. Spread in tin and bake in centre of oven for 45 minutes.

5 Arrange apricots and prune halves alternately in 2 lines down centre and bake for a further 30 to 40 minutes. Test by pressing with fingers. If cooked, cake should spring back, have stopped bubbling and should have begun to shrink from sides of tin.

6 Leave to cool in tin for 5 minutes, then turn out and cool on a wire rack.

---

1 2 3 4 5

PEANUT BRITTLE LAYER CAKE

4oz peanut brittle
3 rounded tablespoons peanut butter
5oz margarine
6oz castor sugar
3 standard eggs
8oz plain flour
1 level teaspoon baking powder
2 tablespoons milk

1 Prepare a cool oven (325 deg F, Gas Mark 3). Grease a deep, round 7in cake tin and line with greaseproof paper; brush paper with oil or melted fat.

2 Place peanut brittle in liquidiser goblet or grinder and run until evenly crushed; place a quarter on one side and remainder in a basin. Add 2 rounded tablespoonsful of peanut butter to crushed brittle in basin and mix well.

3 Place remaining peanut butter in mixer bowl with margarine, cut into pieces; add castor sugar, and run machine until light and fluffy. Add eggs, one at a time, beating well after each addition.

4 Add flour and baking powder to mixer bowl and run machine on lowest setting until well mixed. Add sufficient milk to make a soft dropping consistency.

5 Place half cake mixture in tin; carefully spread peanut butter mixture over to within $\frac{1}{2}$in of edge, then spread remaining cake mixture over; scatter remaining crushed peanut brittle on top.

6 Bake in centre of oven for $1\frac{1}{2}$ hours. Test by pressing with fingers. If cooked, cake should spring back, have stopped bubbling and have begun to shrink slightly from sides of tin. Turn out, remove paper and leave to cool on a wire rack.

Biscuits and Cookies
All of the biscuits pictured here can be quickly made with the help of your mixer. They are: Meringue Crisps, Honey and Peanut Squares, Cherry Krisps, Swiss Biscuit Bars, Oaties, Chocolate Chip Bars, Walnut Cookies, Pinwheel Biscuits, Chocolate Orange Creams, Ginger Cookies and Raisin Rockies

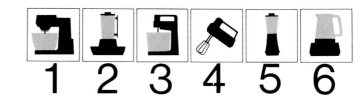

1 3 4   GINGER COOKIES
(pictured left)
Makes about 24:
4oz margarine
3oz castor sugar
3 level tablespoons golden syrup
8oz plain flour
2 level teaspoons ground ginger
2oz rolled oats
1 level teaspoon bicarbonate of soda
1 tablespoon milk

1   Prepare a cool oven (325 deg F, Gas Mark 3). Grease 2 baking sheets.
2   Place margarine, cut into pieces, sugar and golden syrup, in mixer bowl and run machine until mixture is light and fluffy.
3   Add flour, ginger and rolled oats, together with bicarbonate of soda dissolved in milk; run machine until well mixed.
4   Shape into small balls and place on baking sheets, allowing room to spread; flatten slightly with a fork.
5   Bake in centre of oven for 15 to 20 minutes until golden brown. Remove from baking sheets and cool on wire racks.

2 5   CHERRY KRISPS
(pictured left)
Makes 10:
4oz vanilla fudge
3 tablespoons milk
1oz butter
2oz glacé cherries
2 level tablespoons icing sugar
2oz rice krispies

1   Lightly butter a shallow 7in square tin.
2   Cut up fudge and place in a small saucepan with milk; stir over a very low heat until melted.
3   Place in liquidiser goblet. Cut up butter and add to liquidiser, with cherries and icing sugar; run machine until well mixed and cherries are chopped.
4   Place rice krispies in a bowl; pour on fudge mixture and stir until well mixed.
5   Spread mixture in tin and leave to set in a cool place. Cut into 10 bars.

1 3 4   CHOCOLATE ORANGE CREAMS
(pictured left)
Makes about 24 filled biscuits:
4oz margarine
4oz castor sugar
1 standard egg
9oz plain flour
1oz cocoa

FILLING
2oz butter
6oz icing sugar
2 level teaspoons grated orange rind
1 tablespoon orange juice

1   Prepare a cool oven (325 deg F, Gas Mark 3). Grease 2 baking sheets.
2   Place margarine, cut into pieces, and sugar, in mixer bowl and run machine until mixture is light and fluffy. Add egg and beat until well mixed.
3   Add flour and cocoa and run machine until well mixed. Turn out on to a floured board and knead lightly.
4   Roll out dough to $\frac{1}{8}$in thickness; cut into rounds with a $2\frac{1}{4}$in plain cutter. Place on baking sheets, at least $\frac{1}{2}$in apart. Bake in centre of oven for 20 minutes. Allow to cool slightly before removing from baking sheets. Cool completely on wire racks.
5   To make filling: Place butter, cut in pieces, and icing sugar, in mixer bowl. Add grated orange rind and orange juice and run machine until well mixed.
6   When biscuits are cold, sandwich them together with orange filling and dredge with icing sugar.

2 5 6   HONEY AND PEANUT SQUARES
(pictured left)
Makes 16:
8oz plain biscuits
3oz butter or margarine
6 level tablespoons thick honey
4 level tablespoons crunchy peanut butter

1   Lightly butter a shallow 7in square tin.
2   Break biscuits and place, a little at a time, in liquidiser goblet. Run machine until biscuits are coarsely crushed.
3   Place butter in a saucepan. Add honey and bring to the boil, stirring. Remove from heat immediately, stir in the peanut butter, then biscuits, and mix well. Press into tin and leave in a cool place until firm. Cut into 16 squares.

1 3 4   OATIES
(pictured on page 74)

Makes about 20:
2½oz lard
1½oz margarine
3oz castor sugar
1 egg yolk or half a beaten egg
½ teaspoon vanilla essence
4oz self-raising flour
1oz rolled oats

DECORATION
1oz rolled oats
Chocolate beans, glacé cherries, nuts or angelica

1 Prepare a moderate oven (375 deg F, Gas Mark 5). Grease 2 baking sheets.
2 Place fats, cut into pieces, and sugar, in mixer bowl and cream until light and fluffy. Beat in egg and vanilla essence.
3 Add flour and rolled oats and run machine at low speed until well mixed.
4 Roll into walnut-sized balls with wet hands, then dip in rolled oats, to coat.
5 Place on baking sheet, leaving room to spread, and press out slightly. Top each with a chocolate bean, glacé cherry, nut or piece of angelica.
6 Bake in centre of oven for 15 minutes, until pale golden brown. Leave on baking sheets for 5 minutes, then place on a wire rack to cool.

1 3 4   CHOCOLATE CHIP BARS
(pictured on page 74)

Makes 16:
4oz margarine
4oz demerara sugar, 2oz granulated sugar
1 standard egg
1 teaspoon vanilla essence
8oz self-raising flour
½ level teaspoon salt
1 (4oz) packet chocolate chips

1 Prepare a moderate oven (375 deg F, Gas Mark 5). Grease a shallow 7in by 10½in tin.
2 Place margarine, cut into pieces, and sugar, in mixer bowl and cream until light and fluffy. Beat in egg and vanilla essence. Mix in flour and salt at low speed.
3 Stir in chocolate chips; spread mixture in tin. Bake in centre of oven for 30 minutes. Cut into 16 bars; leave to cool slightly, then remove from tin and place on a wire rack to cool.

1 3 4   MERINGUE CRISPS
(pictured on page 74)

Makes about 10:
Rice paper
1 egg white
2oz castor sugar
¾oz cornflakes

1 Prepare a very cool oven (225 deg F, Gas Mark ¼). Line a baking sheet with rice paper.
2 Place egg white in clean, grease-free mixer bowl and whisk until very stiff; add half the sugar and continue whisking until stiff again.
3 Fold in remaining sugar and cornflakes. Place teaspoonsful of mixture on rice paper and bake in coolest part of oven for 1½ to 2 hours, until dry and crisp.

1 3   PINWHEEL BISCUITS
(pictured on page 74 and front cover)

Makes about 20:
3oz margarine
3oz castor sugar
Milk
½ teaspoon vanilla essence
5oz plain flour
1oz cornflour
½ level teaspoon baking powder
2 level teaspoons cocoa

1 Prepare a moderately hot oven (400 deg F, Gas Mark 6). Grease 2 baking sheets.
2 Place margarine, cut into pieces, and sugar, in mixer bowl and run machine at low speed until mixture is light and fluffy. Add 1½ tablespoonsful of milk, vanilla essence, flour, cornflour and baking powder; run machine until well mixed. Remove half mixture and knead on floured board until smooth.
3 Add cocoa and 1 teaspoonful of milk to remaining mixture and run machine until well mixed. Knead until smooth.
4 Roll out each piece of dough to an oblong, 8in by 6in. Brush plain piece with milk, place chocolate piece on top and brush with milk. Starting at a short end, roll up, Swiss-roll fashion.
5 Cut in ¼in slices and arrange on baking sheets, leaving room for them to spread.
6 Bake in centre of oven for about 8 minutes until biscuits are light golden at edges. Remove from baking sheets and leave to cool on a wire rack.

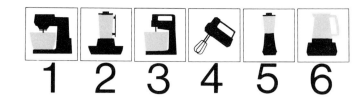

1 3 4   WALNUT COOKIES
(pictured on page 74)

Makes 12:
4oz self-raising flour
4oz soft brown sugar
1½oz cooking fat
2oz shelled walnuts
2oz chocolate chips
1 standard egg

1 Prepare a moderate oven (375 deg F, Gas Mark 5). Grease a baking sheet.
2 Place flour and sugar in mixer bowl, add cooking fat, cut into pieces, and run machine until mixture resembles fine breadcrumbs.
3 Place 12 small, whole walnuts on one side; chop remainder.
4 Add chopped walnuts, chocolate chips and egg to dry ingredients; mix well.
5 Shape into 12 balls and place on baking sheet, allowing room to spread; press lightly with a fork, and place a whole walnut in centre of each.
6 Bake in centre of oven for 10 to 15 minutes, cool slightly on baking sheet, then remove and place on a wire rack.

---

1 3 4   RAISIN ROCKIES
(pictured on page 74)

Makes about 20:
4oz butter
2oz castor sugar
1 egg yolk
½ teaspoon vanilla essence
5oz plain flour
Pinch of salt
2oz seedless raisins

1 Prepare a moderately hot oven (400 deg F, Gas Mark 6). Lightly grease 2 baking sheets.
2 Place butter, cut into pieces, and sugar, in mixer bowl and run machine until mixture is light and fluffy. Mix in egg yolk and vanilla essence, then add flour, salt and raisins.
3 Place mixture in teaspoonsful on baking sheets. Bake in centre of oven for 10 to 12 minutes until lightly browned. Allow to cool slightly before removing from baking sheets. Cool completely on wire racks.

1 3   SWISS BISCUIT BARS
(pictured on page 74 and front cover)

Makes about 12:
8oz butter or margarine
2oz castor sugar
½ teaspoon vanilla essence
8oz plain flour

BUTTER ICING
1oz butter
2oz icing sugar

DECORATION
2oz plain chocolate

1 Prepare a moderate oven (350 deg F, Gas Mark 4). Grease 2 baking sheets. Fill mixer bowl with hot water, place beaters in bowl and leave for 5 minutes; drain and dry.
2 Place butter, cut into pieces, and sugar, in mixer bowl; beat until mixture is light and fluffy. Add vanilla essence and flour and run machine until mixture is smooth and well mixed.
3 Fit a piping bag with a large star tube and fill with mixture. Pipe 4in bars on to baking sheets.
4 Bake in centre of oven for 15 to 20 minutes, until golden brown. Carefully lift biscuits on to a wire rack with a palette knife and leave to cool.
5 To make butter icing: Cream butter and sugar together until smooth. Sandwich biscuits together with butter icing.
6 Break up chocolate and place in a small, dry basin over a saucepan of hot water. Stir occasionally until melted; remove basin from pan.
7 Dip each end of biscuits in chocolate and place on wire rack until set.
NOTE: Biscuit mixture may be piped out into star shapes, swirls and circles and decorated with glacé cherries and angelica. The biscuits can be made up to two weeks in advance, then filled and dipped in chocolate a day or two before they are needed.

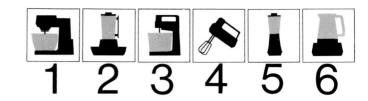

2 5   HAZELNUT GATEAU

2oz shelled hazelnuts
2 standard eggs
4oz castor sugar
4oz butter or margarine
4oz self-raising flour
1 level teaspoon baking powder

BUTTER ICING
8oz icing sugar
3 tablespoons hot water
4oz butter
3 rounded teaspoons hazelnut or chocolate spread

DECORATION
Grated chocolate
A few whole hazelnuts

1 Prepare a moderate oven (350 deg F, Gas Mark 4).
Brush an 8in sandwich tin with oil or melted fat and line
with a circle of greaseproof paper; grease paper.
2 Place nuts in grinder or liquidiser goblet and run for 2 to
3 seconds, until roughly ground; place in a mixing bowl.
3 Place eggs and castor sugar in liquidiser goblet and run
machine until well blended.
4 Cut butter into small pieces, add to mixture in liquidiser
and run machine until well blended.
5 Place flour and baking powder in bowl containing ground
nuts and make a well in centre. Pour in mixture from
liquidiser goblet and stir until well mixed.
6 Turn into prepared cake tin and bake in centre of oven
for about 30 minutes. Test by pressing with fingers. If
cooked, cake should spring back, have stopped bubbling
and have begun to shrink from sides of tin. Turn out,
remove paper and leave to cool on a wire rack.
7 To make butter icing: Place icing sugar in liquidiser,
with hot water, and run machine until blended. Add butter,
cut in small pieces, and hazelnut or chocolate spread, and
run machine for 1 minute. Leave in goblet until set
slightly.
9 Split cake in half horizontally and sandwich with half the
butter icing.
10 Spread sides of cake with butter icing. Hold bottom and
top of cake in hands and dip sides of cake in grated
chocolate.
11 Spread remaining icing over top of cake, swirl with a
knife and decorate with a few whole hazelnuts. Store
gâteau in a cool place.

1 3 4   FANCY ICED CAKES
(pictured right and on front cover)

Victoria Sandwich mixture (see recipe on page 11)
Butter Icing   (see recipe on page 9)
Glacé Icing   (see recipe on page 9)
Individual cake cases

DECORATION
Dolly mixture sweets, small jellied sweets,
chocolate buttons, sugar strands, sugar stars

1 Prepare a moderately hot oven (400 deg F, Gas Mark 6).
Make Victoria Sandwich mixture, as directed on page 11.
2 Place individual cake cases in tartlet tins. Half fill cake
cases with mixture; bake in centre of oven for 15 to 20
minutes. Test by pressing with fingers. If cooked, cakes
should spring back, and have stopped bubbling. Cool on a
wire rack.

To make Butterfly Cakes: Cut a thin slice from top of
each cake and cut it in half. Fold a triangle of greaseproof
paper into a cone. Cut a small piece from bottom and drop
in a star tube. Place a little butter icing in cone and pipe a
circle of icing on each cake. Arrange cake 'wings' in icing
and dust with icing sugar.

To make Top Hats: Cut a circle in top of each cake with a
½in plain piping tube. Fill hole with butter icing and pipe a
swirl on top. Place piece of cake on top and dust with icing
sugar.

To make Cup Cakes: Run glacé icing over cakes and
decorate with a swirl of butter icing; top with a jellied sweet
or chocolate button, or decorate with small jellied sweets,
sugar stars or dolly mixture sweets.

To make Bar Cakes: Prepare a moderate oven (350 deg F,
Gas Mark 4). Brush a shallow, 7in square tin with oil or
melted fat and line base with greaseproof paper; grease
paper. Make up Victoria Sandwich recipe, spoon into tin,
level top and bake for 25 to 30 minutes. Test by pressing with
fingers. If cooked, cake should spring back, have stopped
bubbling and have begun to shrink from sides of tin. Turn
out, remove paper and leave to cool on wire rack. Trim
edges of cake and ice with glacé icing or pipe butter
icing on cake. Cut into 5 bars, then each bar into 3 pieces.
Decorate with sugar strands or piped butter icing and
chocolate buttons, cut into quarters.

Fancy Iced Cakes
These attractive cakes are all made from the basic Victoria Sandwich Cake recipe. The decoration will give you plenty of scope to show your artistic talents

1 3 4　MADELEINES

Makes 12:
4oz margarine
4oz castor sugar
2 standard eggs
4oz self-raising flour
6 tablespoons strawberry jam
2oz desiccated coconut
Strawberries from the jam or glacé cherries

1　Prepare a moderate oven (375 deg F, Gas Mark 5). Grease 12 castle pudding moulds and place on a baking sheet.
2　Place margarine, cut into pieces, and sugar, in mixer bowl and cream together until light and fluffy. Add eggs, one at a time, beating well after each addition.
3　Add flour to creamed mixture and run machine at lowest speed until mixture is just blended.
4　Fill moulds two-thirds full with mixture and bake in centre of oven for 20 minutes, until firm and golden brown.
5　Turn out cakes, invert them on to a wire rack and leave to cool. Trim bases, if necessary, so that they stand upright.
6　Place jam in a saucepan and heat until melted. Remove some whole strawberries for decoration (or use glacé cherries). Hold madeleines, one at a time, on a skewer, brush each with jam and roll in desiccated coconut. Decorate tops with strawberries or glacé cherries.

1 3 4
CHOCOLATE PEPPERMINT RING CAKE

4oz best-quality margarine
4oz castor sugar
3oz self-raising flour
1oz cocoa
1 level teaspoon baking powder
2 standard eggs
2 tablespoons milk

ICING
4oz icing sugar
Boiling water
A little green food colouring
A few drops peppermint essence

Chocolate peppermint creams

1　Prepare a cool oven (325 deg F, Gas Mark 3). Lightly grease a 1½-pint ring jelly mould (or 8in cake tin with cocoa tin weighted with baking beans in centre).
2　Place margarine, cut into pieces, and all other cake ingredients in mixer bowl and run machine until well mixed. Spread mixture evenly in tin and smooth top with a spoon.

3　Bake in centre of oven for 45 minutes. Test by pressing with fingers. If cooked, cake should spring back, have stopped bubbling and have begun to shrink from sides of tin. Turn out on to a wire rack; leave to cool.
4　Sieve icing sugar into a bowl and stir in sufficient boiling water to make a thick icing. Add a little green colouring and and peppermint essence, to taste. Pour over cake allowing icing to run down sides.
5　Decorate cake with chocolate peppermint creams.

1 3 4　APRICOT-GLAZED GATEAU

CAKE
2oz butter
3 standard eggs
1 egg white
4oz castor sugar
4oz plain flour

APRICOT CREAM FILLING
1 large (16oz) can apricot halves
2oz granulated sugar
1 egg yolk
5oz butter, softened

DECORATION
1oz flaked almonds
2 level tablespoons apricot jam
Glacé cherries
Angelica

1　Prepare a moderate oven (350 deg F, Gas Mark 4). Brush bases of 2 (7½in) sandwich tins with oil or melted fat and line each with a circle of greaseproof paper; grease paper.
2　Melt butter in a small basin over a pan of hot water.
3　Place whole eggs, egg white and castor sugar in mixer bowl, and whisk at high speed over a saucepan of hot water on the table, until mixture leaves a trail when mixer is switched off and lifted. Remove bowl from pan and continue whisking until cool. (If using a mixer with a stand and bowl, fill bowl with very hot water, leave for a few minutes, then pour out water and thoroughly dry bowl. Add eggs and sugar to bowl and whisk at high speed until mixture is thick and cool.)
4　Lightly fold in two-thirds of flour with a metal spoon, then melted butter and remaining flour. Pour into prepared tins and bake in the centre of oven for about 40 minutes. Test by pressing with the fingers. If cooked, cakes should spring back, have stopped bubbling and have begun to shrink from sides of tin. Leave to cool in tins for 2 to 3 minutes, then turn out, remove paper and cool on a wire rack.

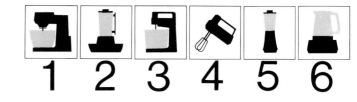

5 Measure 6 tablespoons of apricot syrup from can, place in a small saucepan with granulated sugar. Stir over low heat until sugar has dissolved. Increase heat and boil until syrup reaches 220 deg F on a sugar thermometer, or until syrup forms a thread between 2 teaspoons.

6 Whisk egg yolk in mixer bowl, gradually whisk in sugar syrup and continue to whisk until cold. Cut butter into small pieces and beat into egg mixture, beating well after each addition. Place one third of apricot cream on one side. Brown almonds in oven or under grill.

7 Drain apricot halves, chop three halves and add to larger portion of apricot cream. Sandwich cakes together with this filling. Spread sides of cake with the plain apricot cream and roll in almonds on a sheet of greaseproof paper.

8 Arrange apricot halves on top of cake, rounded sides uppermost. Sieve apricot jam and place in a small saucepan with 1 tablespoon of remaining apricot syrup. Bring just to boil, then spoon over apricots on cake. Arrange half a glacé cherry and 2 angelica 'leaves' between each apricot half around edge of cake.

---

1 3 4   FRUITY BARS

Makes 10:
SHORTCRUST PASTRY
6oz plain flour
½ level teaspoon salt
1½oz margarine
1½oz cooking fat
Cold water to mix

FILLING
5oz dried fruit (currants, sultanas, raisins)
1 to 2 tablespoons marmalade or apricot jam
Castor sugar

1 Prepare a hot oven (425 deg F, Gas Mark 7).
2 Make shortcrust pastry according to directions on page 7. Roll to an oblong and trim edges to measure 10in by 8in. Cut in half to leave 2 pieces, each 10in by 4in.
3 Mix together fruit and marmalade and spread over 1 piece of pastry, leaving a border around edge. Brush border with milk. Cover with other piece of pastry and seal edges. Brush with milk, sprinkle with castor sugar and prick all over with a fork. Mark into 10 bars.
4 Place on baking sheet and bake in the centre of oven for 15 minutes until golden brown.
5 When cold, cut bars.

1 3 4   SEVILLE GATEAU

4oz self-raising flour
1 level teaspoon baking powder
4oz best-quality margarine
4oz castor sugar
2 standard eggs
3 teaspoons milk
½oz desiccated coconut

MARMALADE FILLING
¼ pint water
1oz custard powder
Orange-shred marmalade
½oz butter

---

1 (11oz) can mandarin oranges

1 Prepare a moderate oven (375 deg F, Gas Mark 5). Brush 2 (7½in) sandwich tins with oil or melted fat and line each with a circle of greaseproof paper; grease paper.
2 Place flour and baking powder in mixer bowl, add margarine, cut into pieces, and sugar, eggs and milk. Beat for 1 to 2 minutes until smooth and all ingredients are blended. Divide between tins and smooth tops.
3 Bake in the centre of oven for 20 to 25 minutes until risen and golden brown. Test by pressing with the fingers. If cooked, cakes should spring back, have stopped bubbling and have begun to shrink from sides of tin.
4 Turn out on to a wire rack and remove paper.
5 Place coconut on a baking sheet and brown in oven; leave to cool on a sheet of greaseproof paper.
6 Blend together 1 tablespoon of water and custard powder in a bowl. Put rest of water, with 4 rounded tablespoons of marmalade, in a saucepan and bring to boil, stirring occasionally to break down marmalade. Pour on to custard mixture, stirring. Return to saucepan, bring to boil, stirring continuously; simmer for 2 minutes. Remove from heat; add butter. Leave to cool.
7 Split each cake in half and sandwich halves together with 3 layers of marmalade filling. Warm a little marmalade and brush around sides of cake. Hold bottom and top of cake in hands and dip sides into browned coconut.
8 Brush top of cake with marmalade. Drain mandarin oranges and arrange on cake. Brush over with marmalade to glaze.
NOTE: This cake can be made up to a week in advance, but, once filled, it must be eaten within 2 days.

Sauces, Spreads and Dips

Make up a variety of easily-prepared spreads to take, in little pots, on a picnic, then let everybody make their own sandwiches. In the pots are: Cream Cheese and Nut Spread, Meat Spread and Tuna Spread. Brown sandwiches are filled with Cheese and Anchovy Spread, Cream Cheese and Nut Spread and Tuna Spread. White sandwiches contain Meat Spread and Sardine and Egg Spread

Follow the new method for making smooth, creamy sauces in the liquidiser. Sandwich spreads can be made from left-over meat and fish, while smooth dips will help your parties to go with a swing.

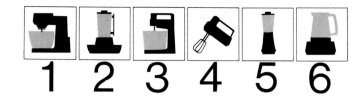

2 5   CHEESE AND ANCHOVY SPREAD

4oz cheese
¼ pint warm milk
Half a (2oz) can anchovies
1 level tablespoon plain flour
¼ level teaspoon pepper
1oz butter

1 Cut cheese into ¾in dice and place in liquidiser goblet together with milk, anchovies, flour and pepper. Run machine until mixture is well blended.
2 Melt butter in a saucepan, add milk mixture and stir over moderate heat until sauce thickens and comes to the boil. Simmer, stirring continuously, for 2 minutes. Pour into a bowl, cover, and leave until cold.
3 Use as a spread for sandwiches (as on back cover) or on toast.

2 5   CREAM CHEESE AND NUT SPREAD

6 tablespoons milk
2oz salted peanuts
6oz cream cheese

1 Place milk and peanuts in liquidiser goblet.
2 Add cream cheese, cut into pieces, and run machine until well blended.
3 Use as a sandwich filling (as on back cover) or spread for cocktail biscuits.

2 5   HOLLANDAISE SAUCE
(pictured on page 47)

2 standard egg yolks
1½ tablespoons lemon juice
Pinch of salt
Pinch of pepper
3oz butter

1 Place yolks, lemon juice and seasonings in liquidiser goblet; run machine until well blended. Heat butter in a small saucepan until foaming but not browned.
2 Pour half the butter into liquidiser and run machine for 5 to 7 seconds or until mixture is well blended. Pour on remaining butter and run machine until mixture thickens and turns creamy yellow.
3 Pour sauce into a basin immediately and keep warm over a pan of hot water until required. Serve with fish or vegetables.

2 5   CHEESE AND TOMATO DIP OR SPREAD
(pictured on back cover)

4oz cheese
¼ pint warm milk
1 level tablespoon plain flour
1 level tablespoon tomato ketchup
¼ level teaspoon salt
¼ level teaspoon pepper
1oz butter
2 tablespoons top of the milk (for dip only)
Chopped parsley (for dip only)

1 Cut cheese into ¾in dice and place in liquidiser goblet together with milk, flour, tomato ketchup, salt and pepper. Run machine until well blended.
2 Melt butter in a saucepan, add milk mixture and stir over a moderate heat until sauce thickens and comes to boil. Simmer, stirring continuously for 2 minutes; remove from heat. For a dip: Beat in top of the milk, pour into a serving bowl, then cover and leave until cold. Serve sprinkled with chopped parsley. For a spread: Cover and leave until cold then use as a spread for sandwiches (as on back cover) or on toast.

2 5   SARDINE AND EGG SPREAD

1 (4½oz) can sardines
2 hard-boiled eggs
1 level tablespoon mayonnaise

1 Place contents of can of sardines in liquidiser goblet. Shell eggs, cut into quarters and add to liquidiser with mayonnaise.
2 Run machine until well mixed, stopping machine and scraping mixture down from sides of goblet, if necessary. Use as a spread for sandwiches.

2   TUNA SPREAD

1 (7oz) can tuna steak
5 level tablespoons mayonnaise (see either recipe on page 12)
2 level teaspoons anchovy essence

1 Place contents of can of tuna in liquidiser goblet with mayonnaise and anchovy essence. Run machine until mixture is smooth, stopping machine and scraping mixture down sides of goblet, if necessary.
2 Use as a spread for sandwiches or on toast.

2 5   MEAT SPREAD

1 small (7oz) can corned beef
7½ fluid oz milk
1 level tablespoon plain flour
¼ level teaspoon pepper
1oz butter
1 beef extract cube

1   Cut corned beef into ½in cubes and place in liquidiser goblet together with milk, flour and pepper. Run machine until mixture is smooth.
2   Melt butter in a saucepan, add meat mixture and beef extract cube, crumbled, and stir over moderate heat until sauce thickens and comes to the boil. Simmer, stirring continuously, for 2 minutes or until beef extract cube has dissolved. Remove from heat, pour into a bowl, cover, and leave until cold.
3   Use as a spread for sandwiches (as on back cover) or on toast.

2 5   CURRIED EGG SPREAD

2 hard-boiled eggs
3 level tablespoons mayonnaise (see either recipe on page 12)
1 level teaspoon curry powder
Salt and pepper

1   Roughly chop eggs; place in liquidiser goblet with mayonnaise and curry powder.
2   Run machine until mixture is smooth. Season to taste.
3   Use as a spread for sandwiches or on toast.

2 5   HAM AND EGG SPREAD

2 standard eggs
2 tablespoons milk
¼ level teaspoon salt
¼ level teaspoon pepper
1oz butter
4oz cooked ham

1   Place eggs, milk, salt and pepper in liquidiser goblet and run machine until well blended.
2   Melt butter in a saucepan; add egg mixture and scramble lightly; return to liquidiser.
3   Cut ham into small pieces and add; run machine until smooth. Pour into a bowl, cover, and leave until cold.
4   Use as a spread for sandwiches or on toast.

2 5   CHICKEN OR TURKEY SPREAD

6oz cooked chicken or turkey
¼ pint milk
1 level tablespoon plain flour
Salt and pepper
1oz butter
1 golden meat extract cube

1   Remove any skin or bone from chicken or turkey and cut into small pieces. Place in liquidiser goblet together with milk, flour and a little salt and pepper. Run machine until smooth.
2   Melt butter in a saucepan, add milk mixture and golden meat extract cube and stir over moderate heat until sauce thickens and comes to the boil. Simmer, stirring continuously, for 2 minutes or until meat extract cube has dissolved. Remove from heat, pour into a bowl, cover, and leave until cold.
3   Use as a spread for sandwiches or on toast.

2 5 6   SWEET AND SOUR SAUCE

Half a green pepper
2 rings canned pineapple
1 medium-sized onion
2 rounded teaspoons cornflour
2 tablespoons pineapple syrup
1 level tablespoon chutney
3 level teaspoons tomato purée
2 teaspoons soy sauce
2 level teaspoons castor sugar
1 tablespoon vinegar
½ pint water
½oz margarine

1   Slice green pepper into strips, discarding seeds, core and white pith. Place in a small saucepan, cover with cold water and bring to boil. Simmer for 3 minutes, then drain. Cut pineapple into pieces. Peel and slice onion.
2   Place cornflour, pineapple syrup, chutney, tomato purée, soy sauce, castor sugar, vinegar and water into liquidiser goblet; run machine until well blended.
3   Melt margarine in a medium-sized saucepan, add onion and cook without browning for 3 minutes.
4   Add mixture from liquidiser. Bring to boil, stirring; cover and simmer for 10 minutes. Add pineapple and green pepper and simmer for a further 5 minutes. Serve hot with pork chops, chicken joints or sausages.

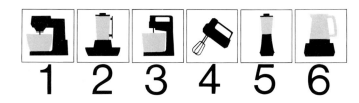

1 2 3 4 5 6

2 5   CELERY AND CHEESE DIP

3oz Cheddar cheese
2 sticks of celery
$\frac{1}{4}$ pint milk
$\frac{1}{2}$oz plain flour
$\frac{1}{2}$oz butter
Salt and pepper

1 Cut cheese into $\frac{3}{4}$in dice and celery into pieces and place in liquidiser goblet with milk and flour. Run machine until celery is finely chopped.
2 Melt butter in a saucepan. Add contents of liquidiser goblet and stir over moderate heat until sauce boils. Simmer, stirring, for 2 minutes. Season to taste. Pour into a serving bowl and leave until cold.

---

2 5   BLUE CHEESE DIP

4oz Danish Blue cheese
$\frac{1}{4}$ pint milk
1 slice raw onion
8oz cottage cheese
$\frac{1}{2}$ level teaspoon salt
Pepper
Paprika or chopped chives (optional)

1 Cut Danish Blue cheese into $\frac{3}{4}$in dice.
2 Place milk and onion in liquidiser goblet and run machine until onion is chopped. Add Blue cheese; run machine until smooth. Add cottage cheese, salt and pepper; run machine until well blended. Pour into a bowl and serve sprinkled with paprika or chopped chives, if desired.

---

2 5   TARTARE SAUCE

$\frac{1}{4}$ pint mayonnaise (see either recipe on page 12)
3 or 4 sprigs parsley
3 gherkins
3 stuffed olives
2 pickled onions (optional)
1 rounded teaspoon capers

1 Place mayonnaise in liquidiser goblet, add parsley and run machine until chopped. Chop gherkins, olives and onions (if used); add to mayonnaise with capers. Run machine for a second until well mixed.
2 Serve with fried or grilled fish.

2 5   LIVER AND BACON SPREAD

8oz lambs' liver
4oz streaky bacon
2oz butter
$\frac{1}{4}$ pint milk
1 level tablespoon plain flour
1 level teaspoon salt
$\frac{1}{4}$ level teaspoon pepper

1 Remove any gristle from liver and cut into pieces. Remove rind and bone from bacon and cut into pieces.
2 Melt 1$\frac{1}{2}$oz butter in a frying pan and gently fry liver and bacon for 8 to 10 minutes. Remove from pan and place on a plate. Cut into small pieces and place in liquidiser goblet.
3 Add juices from pan, milk, flour, salt and pepper and run machine until mixture is smooth.
4 Melt remaining butter in a saucepan, add milk mixture and stir over a moderate heat until sauce thickens and comes to the boil. Simmer, stirring continuously, for 2 minutes. Remove from heat and pour into a bowl; cover and leave until cold.
5 Use as a spread for sandwiches or on toast.

---

2 5   PIQUANT HAM SPREAD

2 standard eggs
2 tablespoons milk
$\frac{1}{4}$ level teaspoon salt
$\frac{1}{4}$ level teaspoon pepper
$\frac{1}{2}$ teaspoon Worcester sauce
$\frac{1}{2}$ level teaspoon dry mustard
1 tablespoon tomato ketchup
1oz butter
4oz cooked ham

1 Place eggs, milk, salt, pepper, Worcester sauce, mustard and tomato ketchup in liquidiser goblet and run machine until well blended.
2 Melt butter in a saucepan, add egg mixture and scramble lightly. Return to liquidiser goblet.
3 Cut ham into small pieces and add; run machine until smooth. Pour into a bowl, cover, and leave until cold.
4 Use as a spread for sandwiches or on toast.

Crab Dip

An unusual way to serve this creamy Crab Dip is to place it in a bowl in a hollowed-out cabbage. Serve savoury biscuits and carrot and celery sticks for 'dunking'

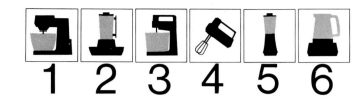

2 5 6   CRAB DIP
(pictured left)
3 level tablespoons natural yoghourt
1 level tablespoon tomato ketchup
1 tablespoon lemon juice
Pinch of Cayenne pepper
$\frac{1}{4}$ level teaspoon salt
6oz cream cheese
1 (7$\frac{1}{2}$oz) can crab meat
1 head of cabbage

1 Place yoghourt, tomato ketchup, lemon juice, Cayenne pepper and salt in liquidiser goblet.
2 Cut up and add cream cheese. Run machine until mixture is smooth.
3 Drain crab meat, discard any tendons and add to liquidiser. Run machine until crab is just chopped.
4 To serve: Place in a small serving bowl or glass dish. Cut out centre of cabbage head, trim stem end so that cabbage will stand firmly and place the bowl in cabbage. Serve crisps, cheese biscuits, carrots and celery sticks for 'dunking'.

---

2 6   HOT CHEESE DIP

8oz Cheddar cheese
1 pint milk
2oz plain flour
$\frac{1}{2}$ level teaspoon curry powder
2oz butter or margarine
1 level dessertspoon tomato purée
Salt and pepper

1 Cut cheese into $\frac{3}{4}$in dice. Place in liquidiser goblet with milk, flour and curry powder, and run machine until cheese is broken down.
2 Melt butter in a saucepan, add cheese mixture and stir over a moderate heat until sauce boils. Simmer, stirring, for 3 minutes. Stir in tomato purée and season to taste.
3 Pour dip into a serving dish and serve with fingers of toast.

2 5 6   TOMATO FONDUE

2 medium-sized onions
6oz Cheddar cheese
3oz margarine
2 large (14oz) cans peeled tomatoes
1 level teaspoon salt
Good pinch of garlic salt
Pepper
$\frac{1}{4}$ teaspoon Worcester sauce
1 rounded tablespoon cornflour

1 Peel and finely slice onions. Cut cheese into $\frac{3}{4}$in dice.
2 Melt margarine in a medium-sized saucepan. Add onion and cook for 3 minutes, until tender.
3 Stir in tomatoes, seasonings and Worcester sauce. Cook, uncovered, for 5 minutes. Cover and simmer for a further 10 minutes.
4 Place half the tomato mixture in liquidiser goblet. Add half the cheese and run machine until fondue is smooth. Repeat with remaining tomato mixture and cheese. Return to pan. Blend cornflour with a little water and add to pan; bring to boil, stirring, and cook for 1 minute.
5 Pour into a warmed fondue pan on a stand over a nightlight or spirit heater. Serve hot and arrange Savoury Bread Cubes (see following recipe) and sticks of carrot and celery in dishes around fondue. Provide cocktail sticks or forks for guests to spear the food and dip into the fondue.
NOTE: If a fondue pan is not available, serve fondue in a small casserole or attractive saucepan.

SAVOURY BREAD CUBES

Makes about 27:
3 (1in thick) slices white bread
3oz margarine
1 level teaspoon curry powder

1 Prepare a moderately hot oven (400 deg F, Gas Mark 6).
2 Remove crusts from bread and cut each slice into 1in cubes.
3 Melt margarine and curry powder in a small bowl over a pan of hot water.
4 Using a skewer or fork, dip bread cubes in melted margarine and turn until well coated. Place cubes on a baking sheet.
5 Bake in oven for 10 to 15 minutes, until crisp and golden brown. Serve hot and spear on to cocktail sticks or forks and 'dunk' in Tomato Fondue.

2 5 6   PARSLEY SAUCE

½ pint Basic White Sauce (see recipe on page 8)
4 or 5 sprigs of parsley

1   Make up white sauce as directed on page 8.
2   Return sauce to liquidiser, add parsley sprigs and run machine until parsley is chopped.
NOTE: When using a large liquidiser, place parsley in liquidiser goblet with milk and flour when making Basic White Sauce. It is then unnecessary to return sauce to liquidiser with parsley.

---

2 5 6   BREAD SAUCE

2oz white bread, with crusts removed
1 small onion
2 cloves
6 peppercorns
½ pint milk
1oz butter
½ level teaspoon salt

1   Break bread into pieces and place, a little at a time, in liquidiser goblet. Run machine until bread is crumbed.
2   Peel and slice onion. Place in a small saucepan with cloves, peppercorns and milk. Cover and leave to infuse over very low heat for 20 to 30 minutes, then strain.
3   Add breadcrumbs, butter and salt and leave in a warm place until bread has swollen. If too thick, add a little top of the milk just before serving.

---

2 5 6   EGG SAUCE

½ pint Basic White Sauce (see recipe on page 8)
2 hard-boiled eggs

1   Make up white sauce, following directions on page 8. Roughly chop eggs.
2   Return sauce to liquidiser goblet, add eggs and run machine until eggs are just chopped.
3   Return sauce to pan and re-heat. Serve with fish.

---

2 5   MINT SAUCE

1 teacupful loosely-packed mint leaves
1 level dessertspoonful castor sugar
4 tablespoons vinegar
2 tablespoons boiling water

Place all ingredients in liquidiser goblet and run machine until mint is chopped.

---

2 5 6   MUSHROOM SAUCE

3oz mushrooms
1½oz margarine
½ pint milk
1oz plain flour
Salt and pepper

1   Wash and slice mushrooms.
2   Melt margarine in a saucepan, add mushrooms and cook slowly for 2 to 3 minutes.
3   Place milk, flour and seasonings in liquidiser goblet and run machine until blended. Add to mushrooms and stir over a moderate heat until sauce boils. Simmer, stirring, for 3 minutes. Serve with chicken or fish.
NOTE: If a smoother sauce is required, return sauce to liquidiser and run machine until mushrooms are chopped. Re-heat before serving.

---

2 5 6   ONION SAUCE

1 large onion
1½oz margarine
½ pint milk
1oz plain flour
Salt and pepper

1   Peel and chop onion, place in a small saucepan with margarine. Cover and cook over a low heat, without browning, for 5 minutes, stirring occasionally.
2   Place milk, flour and seasonings in liquidiser goblet and run machine until well blended.
3   Pour milk mixture into saucepan and stir over a moderate heat until sauce boils. Simmer, stirring, for 5 minutes. Serve with roast lamb.

---

2 5 6   FRESH TOMATO SAUCE

1 small onion
A few celery leaves
½oz margarine
A few bacon rinds
¾lb tomatoes
¼ pint stock or water
Salt and pepper
Pinch of sugar
1 teaspoon tomato purée (optional)
1 level tablespoon cornflour
1 tablespoon cold water

1   Peel and roughly chop onion. Wash celery leaves.
2   Melt margarine in a small saucepan; add onion, celery leaves and bacon rinds and fry for 3 minutes.

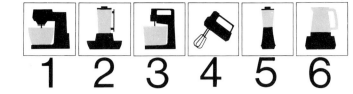

1 2 3 4 5 6

3 Roughly chop tomatoes and add to saucepan with stock, seasonings, sugar and tomato purée (if used). Cover and simmer for 15 minutes, until tomatoes are soft and pulpy.
4 Pour into liquidiser goblet and run machine until blended.
5 Rinse out the saucepan; add cornflour to saucepan and blend with cold water. Strain tomato mixture into saucepan and bring slowly to boil, stirring; simmer for 1 minute. Season to taste and serve hot with fish cakes, fish fingers, beefburgers, rissoles, etc.

---

2 5   FRENCH DRESSING

6 tablespoons olive or vegetable oil
2 tablespoons vinegar
$\frac{1}{2}$ level teaspoon salt
$\frac{1}{4}$ level teaspoon pepper
$\frac{1}{4}$ level teaspoon dry mustard
$\frac{1}{4}$ level teaspoon sugar

Place all ingredients in liquidiser goblet and run machine until well blended. Store in a bottle or covered plastic container. Shake before using.
NOTE: Wine or tarragon vinegar used in French Dressing gives a better flavour than malt vinegar.

---

2 5 6   CHEESE SAUCE

3oz to 4oz cheese
$\frac{1}{2}$ pint milk
1oz plain flour
1oz butter
Salt and pepper

1 Cut cheese into $\frac{3}{4}$in dice. Place cheese, milk and flour in liquidiser goblet and run machine until cheese is broken down.
2 Melt butter in a saucepan, add contents of liquidiser goblet and stir over moderate heat until sauce boils. Simmer, stirring, for 2 minutes. Season to taste.

---

2 5   STRAWBERRY MALLOW SAUCE

1 small ($7\frac{1}{2}$oz) can strawberries
1 (5oz) packet marshmallows

1 Heat strawberries and syrup in a saucepan. Pour into liquidiser goblet, add marshmallows and run machine until well blended.
2 Leave in liquidiser until cold. Run machine for a few seconds, then pour into a jug. Serve on ice cream.

---

2 5 6   APRICOT SAUCE

1 large (15oz) can apricot halves
$\frac{1}{2}$ teaspoon almond essence

Place contents of can of apricots and almond essence in liquidiser goblet. Run machine until well blended. Serve with ice cream.

---

2 5 6   CHOCOLATE SAUCE

$\frac{1}{2}$ pint milk
1 rounded tablespoon cocoa
1 level tablespoon cornflour
3oz granulated sugar

1 Place all ingredients in liquidiser goblet and run machine until well blended.
2 Pour into a saucepan and cook, stirring, over moderate heat until sauce boils. Simmer for 5 minutes, stirring occasionally.

---

2 5 6   LEMON SAUCE

1 lemon
4oz granulated sugar
$\frac{1}{2}$ pint water
1 rounded tablespoon cornflour
Pinch of salt

1 Finely pare rind from half the lemon; place in liquidiser goblet. Cut away white pith and remaining peel, then quarter lemon and place in liquidiser goblet.
2 Add sugar, water, cornflour and salt and run machine until lemon is chopped. Strain into a saucepan.
3 Cook over moderate heat until sauce thickens and boils. Simmer, stirring, for 2 minutes. Serve hot with steamed puddings.

---

2 5   GOOSEBERRY SAUCE

$\frac{1}{2}$lb gooseberries
1oz granulated sugar (or to taste)
2 tablespoons water

1 Remove any leaves from gooseberries, but do not top and tail. Wash fruit, then place in a saucepan with sugar and water. Bring to boil, cover, and simmer for 10 to 15 minutes until fruit is broken down.
2 Place in liquidiser goblet and run machine until sauce is smooth; strain. Serve cold over ice cream or re-heated as an unusual sauce with grilled mackerel.

Drinks

The children will enjoy frothy milk shakes whizzed up in the liquidiser in a trice, while the grown-ups will appreciate the recipes for the more sophisticated drinks.

1 2 3 4 5 6

2 6   ICED COFFEE
(pictured left)
For 4 glasses:
2 level tablespoons instant coffee powder
2 tablespoons boiling water
1 pint milk
1 popular brick vanilla ice cream
Icing sugar (optional)
A little grated chocolate

1 Place instant coffee in a small bowl, add water and stir until dissolved.
2 Place milk and coffee in liquidiser goblet. Cut up and add ice cream. Run machine until mixture is frothy.
3 Pour into glasses, sweeten to taste with icing sugar and top each glass with a little grated chocolate.

2 6   CHOCOLATE COFFEE CLOUD

For 2 glasses:
¾ pint milk
1 standard egg
2 rounded tablespoons drinking chocolate
1 level tablespoon castor sugar
1 level teaspoon instant coffee powder

1 Place milk in a saucepan and bring to boil. Separate egg, place egg yolk in liquidiser goblet and white in a clean, grease-free bowl. Add drinking chocolate to egg yolk, run liquidiser until blended, then add milk and run liquidiser until frothy.
2 Whisk egg white until stiff, then whisk in sugar and coffee powder.
3 Pour chocolate into glasses and pile meringue on top. Serve immediately.

2 6   CARAMEL MILKSHAKE

For 4 glasses:
4oz granulated sugar
Water
1 popular brick vanilla ice cream
1 pint milk

1 Place sugar in a small saucepan with 2 tablespoonsful of water, place over a moderate heat and stir until sugar has dissolved. Bring to boil and cook quickly until sugar caramelises and becomes golden brown in colour.
2 Cool pan in cold water for 2 minutes, then add 4 tablespoons of water. Stir until caramel dissolves.
3 Cut up ice cream and place in liquidiser goblet, add milk and caramel and run machine until well mixed and frothy.
4 Pour into glasses and serve immediately.

2 6   GOLDEN FLIP

For 4 small glasses:
1 small (8oz) can apricot halves
3 tablespoons rosehip syrup
¾ pint milk

1 Place contents of can of apricots, rosehip syrup and milk in liquidiser goblet.
2 Run machine until apricots are well blended and mixture is frothy. Pour into glasses and serve immediately.

2 5 6   APRICOT FIZZ

For 4 glasses:
1 small (8oz) can apricot halves
1 strip thinly-pared lemon rind
Soda water, bitter lemon or lemonade

1 Place contents of can of apricots in liquidiser goblet. Add lemon rind and run machine until apricots are smooth.
2 Divide between glasses and top up with soda water, bitter lemon or lemonade.

2 6   BUTTER-CHOC SHAKE

For 4 small glasses:
1 pint milk
4 level dessertspoons butterscotch instant whip
4 level teaspoons drinking chocolate

1 Place all ingredients in liquidiser and run machine until well blended.
2 Leave for 5 minutes, then pour into glasses.

2 6   STRAWBERRY MILKSHAKE
(pictured on front cover)
For 3 glasses:
¼lb strawberries
¾ pint milk
1 popular brick vanilla ice cream

1 Wash and hull strawberries and place in liquidiser goblet with milk. Cut up and add ice cream.
2 Run machine until strawberries are broken down and mixture is frothy.
3 Pour into glasses and serve immediately.

RASPBERRY MILKSHAKE

Substitute raspberries for strawberries and strain into glasses, to remove pips.

2 5 6   VEGETABLE JUICE COCKTAIL

For 2 glasses:
2 or 3 sprigs watercress
1 sprig parsley
Half a stick of celery
2 tomatoes
Small piece of cucumber
Thin slice of peeled onion
Scant $\frac{1}{4}$ pint water
Salt and pepper

1 Wash vegetables and trim celery. Cut tomatoes and cucumber into small pieces.
2 Place all vegetables and water in liquidiser goblet and run machine until blended.
3 Pour through a strainer into a jug. Season to taste. Pour into glasses and serve.
NOTE: Any fresh vegetables can be added to this mixture; it can be seasoned with garlic or celery salt, if desired.

2 5 6   ST. CLEMENT'S REFRESHER

For 4 glasses:
1 large orange
2 lemons
Water
1$\frac{1}{2}$oz to 2oz castor sugar

1 Remove peel and pith from orange and lemons. Cut into quarters and remove centre pith.
2 Place fruit in liquidiser goblet, run machine until well blended and strain into a measuring jug. Add water to make 1 pint. Sweeten to taste with sugar.

2 5 6   CARLTON COOLER

For 4 glasses:
1 orange
1 small (8oz) can crushed pineapple
Lemonade

1 Wash orange, cut 4 thin slices from orange and put on one side. Cut two thin strips of rind from remainder of orange and place in liquidiser goblet.
2 Cut remaining peel and pith from orange and discard. Cut orange into pieces and add to liquidiser.
3 Add contents of can of pineapple and run machine until pineapple is well blended. Press through a coarse sieve into a jug. Divide between glasses and top up each glass with lemonade.
4 Cut each of reserved orange slices from centre to rind and place on rim of each glass. Serve immediately.

2 5 6   STRAWBERRY FIZZ

For 4 glasses:
6oz strawberries
2 level tablespoons castor sugar
Soda water

1 Wash and hull strawberries and place in liquidiser goblet with sugar and 3 to 4 tablespoonsful of soda water.
2 Run machine until strawberries are smooth. Divide between glasses. Top up each glass with soda water.

2 6   EGG NOG

For 2 glasses:
$\frac{3}{4}$ pint milk
Few drops vanilla essence
1 level tablespoon castor sugar
1 standard egg
Pinch of ground nutmeg

1 Place milk in a small saucepan and bring just to the boil.
2 Place vanilla essence, sugar and egg in liquidiser goblet and run machine until just blended. Pour on milk and run machine until frothy. Pour into glasses and sprinkle with a very little nutmeg.

2 5 6   INDIVIDUAL MILKSHAKES

General instructions:
Place all ingredients in liquidiser goblet, first cutting up any fruit and ice cream, and run machine until well blended. Pour into a glass and serve.

HAZELNUT MILKSHAKE

2 rounded teaspoons hazelnut spread
$\frac{1}{2}$ pint milk

HONEY MILKSHAKE

2 level teaspoons clear honey
$\frac{1}{2}$ pint milk

BLACKCURRANT MILKSHAKE

2 tablespoons bottled blackcurrant syrup
$\frac{1}{2}$ pint milk
1 brickette vanilla ice cream

BANANA MILKSHAKE

1 ripe banana, peeled and cut up
Scant $\frac{1}{2}$ pint milk

Sweeten to taste, if necessary, and served with grated chocolate on top.

Index

First published in 1968
by FAMILY CIRCLE
Elm House Elm Street London WC1
4th Reprint 1971
Printed in the Netherlands by
Smeets Lithographers Weert
© Standbrook Publications Ltd 1968
A Member of The Thomson Organisation Ltd